T5-CPY-498

POPE PIUS XII LIBRARY, ST. JOSEPH COL.

3 2528 06300 3562

TRANSFORMING
MIDDLE SCHOOLS

HOW TO ORDER THIS BOOK

BY PHONE: 800-233-9936 or 717-291-5609, 8AM-5PM Eastern Time

BY FAX: 717-295-4538

BY MAIL: Order Department
Technomic Publishing Company, Inc.
851 New Holland Avenue, Box 3535
Lancaster, PA 17604, U.S.A.

BY CREDIT CARD: American Express, VISA, MasterCard

TRANSFORMING MIDDLE SCHOOLS
A GUIDE TO WHOLE-SCHOOL CHANGE

BARRY RAEBECK

TECHNOMIC
PUBLISHING CO., INC.
LANCASTER · BASEL

Transforming Middle Schools
a **TECHNOMIC**®publication

Published in the Western Hemisphere by
Technomic Publishing Company, Inc.
851 New Holland Avenue
Box 3535
Lancaster, Pennsylvania 17604 U.S.A.

Distributed in the Rest of the World by
Technomic Publishing AG

Copyright © 1992 by Technomic Publishing Company, Inc.
All rights reserved

No part of this publication may be reproduced, stored in a
retrieval system, or transmitted, in any form or by any means,
electronic, mechanical, photocopying, recording, or otherwise,
without the prior written permission of the publisher.

Printed in the United States of America
10 9 8 7 6 5 4 3

Main entry under title:
    Transforming Middle Schools: A Guide to Whole-School Change

A Technomic Publishing Company book
Bibliography: p. 177
Includes index p. 181

Library of Congress Card No. 92-64255
ISBN No. 0-87762-958-7

CONTENTS

PREFACE

*What is now prov'd, was
once only imagin'd.*
—WILLIAM BLAKE

Successful people are idealistic. They believe in noble and grand principles. They believe that what they are doing, day by day, is an essential, even spiritual work. Effective educators are no different. The strong ones are the ones who attempt to connect with every single child. They are the ones who have personally known the magical power of human transformation. They have enabled others to exceed all expectations, all odds—and they want to replicate that success again and again. They know that human potential is a great and inexplicable force, always capable of far more than the statistics, the "realists," the prognosticators, and the past can predict.

Successful organizations are also idealistic. The central issue in educational transformation at any level is the one so rarely even mentioned—the issue of spirit. The void at the center of mediocre and ineffective classrooms, schools, and school systems is a spiritual one. In order to be fully productive and alive we need to feel that what we are doing, day by day, is essential. In a thriving organization we believe as one body that our goal is a mission, that our mission is a grand and noble one, and that we are somehow, in some way, moving ever closer to realizing that vision.

ACKNOWLEDGEMENTS

A work of this type is based on a great deal of experience with a lot of wonderful people over a long time period. I am especially indebted to former Thomas Harrison Middle School colleagues Tim Frazier, Tracy Neyhart, Judy Bland, Gayle Frye, Sandy Crenshaw, Dick Hahn, Jack Smith, Ellen Lucius, Paul Clifford, Steve Doyle, and Tamesa Williams, among many others. We worked hard, thought much, grew tremendously, and had great fun going from a good school to a great school.

I would like to thank the fine and professional staff at Technomic for assisting me in all phases of the publishing process. Joe Eckenrode, Susan Farmer, and Douglas Bishop were particularly instrumental. They have been patient, thoughtful, thorough, and kind throughout.

Many great thinkers have inspired me over the years. Among them I must include William Blake, Chuang Tzu, A. N. Whitehead, John Dewey, and Ralph Waldo Emerson. Of our more modern writers and thinkers focusing on American education I would mention Paul George, Howard Johnston, John Goodlad, Ernest Boyer, Ted Sizer, Charles Silberman, and Mortimer Adler.

Finally I would like to thank my family. My father, Charles Raebeck, has been a champion of educational, social, and personal transformation for fifty years now. My wife, Susan Leslie Raebeck, a fine teacher in her own right, has been as loving and supportive as one person can be. My daughters, Tessa, Annabel, and Emily, through their unending joy, exuberance, and beauty, continually make every effort worthwhile. Thank you all.

INTRODUCTION

WHAT TOM TOLD ME

When I arrived my first summer to become principal of Tom Jasper's junior high school, he was one of a few teachers who made a point of coming in to see me. He was tall, well-spoken, and clearly intelligent. Tom was a leader with little following, for the school wasn't designed that way. And he had serious concerns.

He was frustrated with so many of the typically thoughtless practices of the school. And he was frustrated that so many good things had come and gone over the years. Several fine and effective practices (such as teaming and interdisciplinary units) had simply disappeared through a lack of focus and commitment by administrators and staff.

Tom told me that his patience with his students, especially the boys, was thinner than it once was. He was spending less time at school than he used to. After years of success he was even thinking of giving up coaching the basketball team. Tom said that the kids in the school were not as respectful as they used to be and that they did not care as much either. He also felt he was not getting the support from the administration that he once got.

Tom taught his classes in isolation. Rarely, if ever, did any adult come in to observe, or just to enjoy his teaching. He did his planning alone as well, with little professional dialogue. His curriculum had remained essentially the same for many years; his tests and his assignments had not changed much in a while either. Many student-centered concepts had been introduced, then abandoned. Tom was actually looking toward retirement for the first time. As an entity, this traditional school was growing as tired, irritable, and frustrated as Tom.

The school staff was struggling with a new generation of students unlike any they had seen before. The city had grown tremendously in a short time and had annexed surrounding land that included three federally subsidized housing projects. The demographics were not the same as that conservative middle-class community had always known. Suddenly the school had 25% of its students on free and reduced lunch and textbooks, and a good many more not much above the cutoff. All the destructive national patterns of divorce, poverty, substance abuse, violence, theft, malnourishment, sexual abuse, homelessness, disease, and illiteracy were manifest in that junior high school population.

Unable to establish appropriate attitudes and effective systems, with little or no support or leadership for staff development and innovation, the staff had fallen into an adversarial role with a large percentage of its students. Five academic levels had been established, effectively tracking the kids into segregated groups, even in physical education. The dropout rate was 5% (in seventh and eighth grade!), the retention rate was 9% (with many students spending four years in a two-year program), 22% of all students failed one or more courses for the year, discipline referrals, detentions, and suspensions were at all-time highs, and the school yearbook was entitled *Off the Wall*. The school was getting closer and closer to being out of control.

Those were powerful concerns. But along with them Tom also had ideas. The more he spoke the more evident it became that he was itching to do things differently. Listening to Tom I learned several things. One was that the problem was more intensely pressing than I had realized. Another was that many other people on the staff were anxious to help, possessing great amounts of often untapped energy and resourcefulness. Another was that Tom would make a great team leader—once we got ourselves into teams. And yet another was that I liked Tom a great deal and respected him immediately. I knew that we could work well together and have fun in the process.

SOLUTIONS BECOMING FADS

There is great national interest on the part of teachers, parents, legislators, business people, administrators, professors, students, and citizens in making our middle-level schools, and all our schools, more productive and simultaneously more humane. There is no shortage of solid research and strong study delineating why we need improvement and what needs improving. There is also no shortage of specific methods for improvement (cooperative learning, peer coaching, inter-disciplinary curriculum, assertive discipline, teacher-student advisory, etc.) and broad outlines for improvement (effective schools, site-based management, outcome-based education, parental choice, the President's goals, etc.).

The constant danger, of course, is that these elements taken independently and haphazardly rarely produce lasting improvement. They are more likely to be short-term solutions or, still worse, merely fads. What is all too often lacking is a synthesis of theory and practice at the school level. A thoughtful synthesis, supported by energetic leadership and committed staff, can result in the creation of a full range of congruent, specific practices set on a clear, meaningful philosophical/theoretical foundation. That is a fancy way of saying that good ideas brought to life and sustained by creative people make for excellent schools.

We have excellent schools now—we do not do enough to celebrate them. We also have excellent programs within good, mediocre, and poor schools—we don't do enough to share those programs. This book is not about school- or education-bashing, although it does not go easy on senseless practices. It is about transformation of weak programs to good ones, of good ones to great ones. It is about daring to be great.

We adopted a slogan during my first year: "*A Good School Becoming a Great School!*" Some loved it and were enthralled with the challenge. Others were offended because they didn't care to admit the school was not "great" already. But we insisted that "greatness" was not a cheap commodity, not a thing easily attained. After three years of massive growth/improvement efforts we still may not have been great—although 350 educators came to visit us our third year to decide for themselves. But it was clear to anyone who cared to look, to feel, and to check the data, that we were a heckuva lot closer to greatness and far better for our efforts, professionally and personally.

MEAT

As you know, school people are not vegetarians. What school people continually hunger for is meat: specific, sensible practices that can be implemented on-site, in the classroom. Yet school people, like Tom Jasper, have long since grown weary of the quick-fix approach. We know that meaningful improvement, even daring to be great, doesn't come cheap. We also know investing time and energy in pendular panaceas year after year is terribly fruitless. We want to be able to see the potential value of a change—and to the degree that it becomes clear we *will* make the necessary investment of time and energy.

This book will outline a host of strategies, systems, and procedures that *really work*. These may be adapted independently to supplement what you are already doing, or they may be embraced more fully in what I call a "whole-school approach." However, by taking a whole-school approach grounded in learning theory and democratic belief, we can move to genuine middle-level transformation. Travelling through this process is designed to enable you to have a lasting growth/improvement (G/I) impact on your program and/or ones that you work with.

THE WHOLE-SCHOOL APPROACH

The rationale for a whole-school approach also rests in the fundamental inadequacy of piecemeal, fragmented, isolated attempts at school improvement. If one were to walk into a corporation with the mission of improving it, it is unlikely that the approach would focus solely on leadership, or personnel, or quality control, or public relations. In order to be fully successful in implementing substantive G/I over a long period of time, one would have to look at the corporation holistically. Then if it were apparent that the leadership was weak and the public relations were strong, energy would obviously be directed at improving leadership capability. This effort is not effective in isolation however. If too much attention is given solely to leadership, it is probable that in time public relations will suffer.

Problems will emerge in a cyclical fashion if they are dealt with in a cyclical fashion. It may prove more strenuous and more challenging to take a whole-system approach (or whole-school approach in our case), yet it is bound to be more beneficial and lasting in the long run. One reason school changes tend not to be particularly productive is the very nature of their piecemeal implementation. How effective is it to introduce more positive grading practices without looking at our grouping practices? How effective is it to attempt to make the school a better place for the students without attempting to improve it for adults as well? How can we make our schedule more whole without linking this to curriculum?

GENESIS OF MIDDLE SCHOOL EDUCATION

The middle school movement began in the early 1960s as a thoughtful antidote to the junior high school. The junior high school was just that, a miniature high school, generally encompassing grades seven to nine. That format was perhaps an improvement over grade seven to twelve schools, but in time it was seen to be inadequate in fully answering the needs of the pre-adolescent and early adolescent (or transescent) young person.

In addition, as physical and social maturation patterns sped up in the culture during this century, it was noticed that the typical sixth grader was inappropriately placed in a K–6 environment. The middle school, housing grades six to eight, was designed to deal more effectively with the total person, this complex and developmentally unique transescent going through some of the most dramatic physical and psychosocial maturational changes of a lifetime during those few years (Elkind, 1980; Glatthorn and Spencer, 1986; Lipsitz, 1980).

What arises from this thinking are programs designed to accept and allow for the current development levels of the students; provide a rich, engaging, and appropriate experience; and operate fully and meaningfully in the four domains: the intellectual, physical, social, and psychoemotional or spiritual.

As will be discussed in detail throughout this book, the notion of attempting to educate and encourage the whole child is not a new idea, nor is it restricted to middle-level programs. It is all too obvious, however, that we lack full acceptance of this notion long espoused by our most thoughtful and respected educators, people such as Ralph Waldo Emerson, John Dewey, Maria Montessori, Jean Piaget, Alfred North Whitehead, John Goodlad, Jerome Bruner, and Benjamin Bloom, to name several. Such acceptance remains far from a reality in our schools or the larger society somewhat tenuously supporting them.

TENETS OF MIDDLE SCHOOL EDUCATION

It is not necessary that your school be called a "middle school" in order for it to be good, or even great. As we know there are too many schools that have taken the title of "middle school" without incorporating a fraction of the philosophy or program of a true middle school. They are just those old junior high schools in disguise. And there are "junior high" and "intermediate" schools with terrific "middle school" orientation and programs. Let us not get hung up on the name. Let us focus instead on several elements seen in the best middle-level schools.

(1) *Teaming:* of staff in small groups (two to five) able to teach the four major subjects of language arts, science, math, and social studies; of students in groups of 50–125 housed as a unit in the building, all working with the same team of teachers for at least one year.

(2) *Whole-Child Approach:* all aspects of the student's being (intellectual, physical, social, and psychoemotional) are considered in structuring the teaching/learning program along developmentally appropriate lines.

(3) *Advisory Program:* each student in the school is part of a subgroup of ten to fifteen students who are the direct responsibility of one staff member who is a "significant other" to them, and with whom they meet daily in a homeroom setting and at least once a week for a longer period of time.

(4) *Integrated Curriculum:* there is a conscious, continuous attempt by the teaching staff to make the curriculum as whole, interdisciplinary, and relevant to the lives of the students as possible.

(5) *Block Schedule:* the daily schedule provides for larger, flexible blocks of "core" time to be used as the interdisciplinary team sees fit.

(6) *Exploratory Arts Program:* there is provision for all students to experience the practical and fine arts throughout each year through an elective/exploratory program.

(7) *Cooperative, Competitive, and Autonomous Activities:* all students have ample opportunities to succeed in a variety of activities, groups, structures, and settings tailored both to current ability and unknown potential.

(8) *Dynamic, Engaging Teaching/Learning Experiences:* the class-room is at least as compelling as any other facet of the strong middle-level program.

(9) *Committed, Visionary Leadership and Staff:* no program will succeed in transformation without open, upbeat people!

NOTE: Every one of these tenets is applicable at elementary and secondary levels, as well as the middle level. Not only are they applicable — they are desirable. It would be terrific for our national education system if more of these middle-level concepts would be incorporated into the two other levels also. This would help arrest the alarming trend of the "secondary-ation" of elementary programs. This unhealthy trend translates into more classes, more teachers, more grouping, more schedule changes, and more fragmentation of the teaching/learning experience at lower and lower levels. It would be far healthier for our ineffectual, increasingly obsolete high school programs to adopt the best primary school methods and structures than for the elementary schools to adopt high school structures long proven inadequate (Boyer, 1983; Goodlad, 1984; Sizer, 1984).

FUSION

Isolated attempts are not going to do it, theoretical study is not going to do it, in-service is not going to do it, money is not going to do it, better teacher/administrator training programs are not going to do it, parental involvement is not going to do it, miraculous intervention from above is not going to do it — although *all* of these things can be part of doing it. What is required is a long view, a sustained commitment, an intensely thoughtful approach, and a truly spiritual, egalitarian attitude. All of this must be fused with definitive, practical, user-friendly systems that can be implemented in any variety of ways. This book is a map — it is *not* a blueprint. In the Appendix are outlined one-, three-, and five-year procedures for transformation. It is wise to caution against blanket adaptations, however, as thoughtful educators will need to tailor the suggestions to their situation.

I hope many of you will say, "Hey, we do *that* already, that's no big deal." These concepts and systems are both original and borrowed, developed thoughtfully and on the fly, based on theory and on practice—ours and other people's. What was perhaps unique about our school was the way in which so many ideas became effective systems—and in a relatively short time frame. Once people are freed up, incredible synergy results—and G/I accelerates dramatically, gaining a life of its own.

Future change acceptance is proportional to current change effectiveness. That means that when staff, students, and community see things working better, they become more open to attempt further change. Change has to be seen as G/I, not simply change. Thus early changes should be substantive, practical, and sustained. First get the restrooms clean—then try a little teaming pilot. First get the copier working—then try a little cooperative learning. First set a positive tone—then begin transformation.

And remember, "Life is a game to be played, not a problem to be solved." If it is not fun at least some of the time, it probably is not good and it definitely will not last.

1

PRAGMATIC IDEALISM IN A CHAOTIC, FRAGMENTED AMERICA

He who knows he has enough is rich.
— CHUANG TZU, 300 B.C. or so

SCHOOLS AS MUSEUMS

Not enough time. Not enough money. Not enough meaning. Not enough. We thirst for more, always more. What advertisers exploit as a material thirst is actually a physical manifestation of a deeper thirst.

In an age of new limitations, Americans are anxious. In an age of dwindling resources, Americans are still unable to save. In an age requiring dramatic new vision, Americans elect leaders who promise a return to a time that never existed. In an era necessitating serious thought, Americans rent foolish videos. Our paradigms are being shifted for us, not by us.

In our schools it is often the same. The entire world is in flux and school personnel argue whether to fail kids with a 75 or a 70. The international communist movement disintegrates in six months and school boards debate whether or not human artistic expression is a frill. Global economies respond in microseconds to macrolevel monetary shifts and school boards cut money for computers because, "They already have computers." Japan and Germany are killing us in large measure because we are unable to function in interdependent teams in the workplace — and elitist parents are convinced despite all evidence to the contrary that cooperative learning will be the end of Western civilization as we now know it.

Schools are museums, light years behind the rest of the culture in terms of technology, responsiveness, and awareness of how modern life moves. Too many schools function as though children are essentially mindless, teachers are larger kinds of children, thinking is some element of "curriculum design," intelligence can be quantified with a #2 pencil, teaching/learning is "instruction to be delivered," and spirit is a thing only cheerleaders possess.

Schools perpetuate inane, fragmenting, or obsolete practices often for no other reason than "That's the way we've always done it." Tom Peters, the celebrated author of *Thriving on Chaos*, says, "If it ain't broke—fix it anyway!" The Japanese have an awareness called "kaizen," which means "constant improvement." In our schools we are still

- ringing bells that "fire alarm" the school ten times a day
- disrupting a thousand people on the PA to find a custodian
- herding hundreds of kids into cafeterias for forty-five minute periods, expecting them to be "quiet"
- grading kids the first week of a school year
- quizzing and testing kids to death with no real benefit
- tracking kids beginning in first grade
- denying and/or monitoring teachers' phone use
- making teachers sign in and out
- plodding through textbooks to "cover the content"
- applauding mediocre student effort
- posting all the grades on the wall
- keeping boys in from recess because they are too active
- putting teachers into teams but not providing common planning time
- treating parents like suspicious intruders
- having students take eight to ten different courses with eight to ten different teachers in eight to ten different locations *each day*
- retaining kids *one year* for failing *one subject*
- not permitting students to collaborate in their work
- not telling students what it is we expect them to learn
- blaming everyone but ourselves for what is happening
- (your choice) _____

MEANWHILE . . .

We are becoming a two-tiered society. We may already have become one. The middle class has eroded to such a degree that the median household income ($33,000 in 1990) is inadequate to provide upward mobility in most communities. The gap between the wealthy and the poor grew substantially during the 1980s. A greater concentration of wealth is in the hands of fewer Americans than ever before. We have the most unequal distribution of wealth of any industrialized nation. Our health care system is a mess, with tens of millions of Americans unable to afford protection. One in five children lives in poverty. Millions more live in a low-income world just above that terrible zone.

The violence, ugliness, and fear of the barren, dirty inner city is beyond anything Stanley Kubrick portrayed in his *A Clockwork Orange*, written nearly thirty years ago. That film's X rating would probably get a PG now, and that is part of our problem too. Automatic weapons are available through magazine order, as if that were some inalienable right assigned by the founding fathers. The NRA and the gun merchants behind them block every effort to establish some form of sanity as America functions more and more like an armed and hostile camp. We have a far higher percentage of our populace in prison than any other industrialized nation—and we can not build new prisons fast enough. More black males of college age are in prison than in college. Hundreds of thousands of impoverished, illiterate, often deranged American men and women drift alone in our cities begging, waiting, crying, and dying. Sensitive Americans feel helpless and ashamed.

AND BACK TO OUR SCHOOLS . . .

We hit the limits apparently in the 1960s when we reached the 75% graduation rate for high schools. After decades of improvement in that rate, we have been unable to progress. What's more, in the inner cities the rate is often not even 50%. In an information society, should we even use high school graduation as a bellwether? Is not college graduation a more important statistic, a greater indicator of our ability to fully educate our youth? In reality the high school diploma in and of itself has had virtually no value for years. Students have recognized this a lot sooner than educators or parents. High school diplomas are only good as a ticket to college. Employers of non-college graduates rarely even inquire about them.

In comparison to other developed nations, even our strongest students often do not measure up. As a group our students are usually among the lowest ranked no matter what the subject or the test. I would suggest here that in terms of their affinity for learning and belief in the *inherent* value of education our students and our citizens generally would rate very low as well. America has long been a fundamentally utilitarian culture, one that has rarely valued scholarship or intellectual inquiry for its own sake. It is a nation traditionally suspect of schooling and of educators, never according teachers a great deal of respect or sustenance, rarely placing schools in high regard, generally suspicious of theory, wary of poetry, skeptical of the place of the arts in a productive life.

But it may be this stubborn belief in practicality, this enduring emphasis on the bottom line that will prove to be our salvation. America takes a long time to focus on an issue of concern. Once it does, however, it can galvanize will and resources as dramatically as any nation, and often to wondrous effect. America remains a vital and great nation. And America is slowly coming to realize that it had better establish and *maintain* a focus on improving our educational systems.

Obviously education can be one of the few solutions to our social problems — not education per se, however, and not educational "reform" (oh, that tired little six-letter word). *Transformation*, not reformation, is required. We need education that is whole, thoughtful, humane, rigorous, idealistic, and tremendously practical. What we need now is a wedding of sound theory and proven practice. We need "*pragmatic idealism*." And what we need does not cost money.

ATTITUDE

It is a matter of attitude:

- the attitude that learning is inherently meaningful
- the attitude that teaching is a noble, spiritual calling
- the attitude that joy and rigor are not polar opposites
- the attitude that all children can learn — all children
- the attitude that all children deserve equal access to the means and processes of education — all children
- the attitude that maintaining high expectations for lower-class and/or minority kids is not racism, it is just the opposite

Racism (classism) is expecting and accepting less from lower-class and/or minority kids in terms of productivity and in terms of behavior.

Racism (classism) is allowing lower-class and/or minority kids to stumble along and not help them lift themselves up. Racism is having double standards in the name of "not being too tough on them."

Strong educators have long known that students conform to our expectations. Believers have always known that miracles happen when we expect them to. Students are not the same; not all will go on to great academic heights, nor need they. But as Luis Alberto Machado states in his work of the same name, every student has *"The right to be intelligent."* Every student who comes to us has the right to gain as much access to knowledge and experience as he/she possibly can. Will this come about easily? Machado says, "If there has been steely resistance to the democratization of government, it will be even stronger towards the democratization of talent."

We do not have to go into inner-city schools to see human potential wasted. You could visit a wealthy suburban middle level or high school full of well-behaved, well-heeled kids and still see hundreds who feel restless, bored, inadequate, anxious, underutilized, ignoble. According to several lengthy studies of secondary schools in America, the greatest problem in them is not violence, not drugs, not even discipline; it is boredom (Boyer, 1983; Goodlad, 1983; Sizer, 1984). Every student has the right to leave each and every school feeling that he/she is valuable, capable, and optimistic about life's promise, whatever the particular direction chosen.

That right may be forfeited through consistently aberrant, disruptive, or violent behavior—but only when thoughtful, sensitive, and powerful interventions have been tried and have not worked. It should never be forfeited because of lowered expectations and senseless school practices, like tracking, that lead to the diminishing of dreams (George, 1988).

2

TOWARD WHOLENESS: TEACHING/LEARNING, JOY/RIGOR, AND PROCESS/PRODUCT

> *The true state of affairs in the material world*
> *is wholeness. If we are fragmented, we*
> *must blame it on ourselves.*
> *—DAVID BOHM, PHYSICIST*

THE DICHOTOMIC DANGER

It seems that we still think in dichotomies. Despite John Naisbitt's prediction in *Megatrends* over a decade ago that Either/Or thinking would give way to Multiple Options thinking, we are having trouble breaking out of the black/white mold. Our thinking, in the larger culture and perhaps even more so in education, is very much structured by the mechanistic, dualistic, deterministic patterns popular in the West since Aristotle. This was continued and refined by Aquinas, Newton, and Descartes, among others. It was then taken to perhaps absurdist extremes regarding human behavior and intelligence by behavioral psychologists such as E. L. Thorndike, George Yerkes, and Edward Terman in the early twentieth century, and of course B. F. Skinner at mid-century (Caine and Caine, 1991; Gould, 1985; Phillips and Soltis, 1985).

Thorndike extrapolated huge theories on human intelligence from his work shocking frightened cats in darkened boxes. We bought it. Terman and Yerkes got hold of Binet's work on diagnostic testing in France, testing that was only used for remediation, and then used it for exactly what Binet feared and deplored most—IQ testing. These tests were first used on Army recruits in World War I. Hundreds of soldiers, many illiterate, would be given pencils and told to go to it under crowded, timed, extremely stressful conditions. (How would you like to take one test that determined whether you would be in the trenches or in the officer corps?) We are still doing equally senseless things to our schoolchildren. Labelling second grade students Gifted/Talented

7

on the basis of one IQ test is a widespread example (more on that in Chapter 10).

We have not really integrated the thinking of Einstein and his Theory of Relativity in 1905, let alone Heisenberg's Uncertainty Principle of 1926, which led to the formulation of quantum mechanics. Quantum mechanics does not predict a single, definite result for an observation; rather it may predict several possible outcomes, some more likely than others. Quantum mechanics has also noted the wave/particle duality: that there is no real distinction between the two—particles may sometimes behave like waves, and waves sometimes may behave like particles, depending on conditions.

David Bohm, Stephen Hawking, and other modern physicists are patiently explaining that our world is not at all what we think it is. Determinism is a woefully simplistic notion in a universe where time is curved. Either/Or doesn't help us much in a universe where

- simple pattern/simple chaos
- complex pattern/complex chaos
- infinite pattern? infinite chaos?

might be the way systems work—some systems. It no longer serves us in our extraordinarily rapid-fire, real-time world. We must be increasingly versatile and fluid in our thinking. We must develop what Tom Peters and others call a "high tolerance for ambiguity." We must move from the narrowly dualistic to the broadly holistic. Or is this, too, an overly simple dichotomy?

BUILDING ON WHAT WE KNOW

When we look at the current phenomenon of Cooperative Learning in the nation's classrooms, there is cause for both delight and concern: delight because it may provide a balance to the overly competitive and autonomous experiences long dominant; concern because the way we typically handle innovations of this type is to embrace them totally and exclusively. This will lead to a study in several years showing that American students can no longer work independently or competitively

—and we will go roaring "back to basics" again in separate rows and desks!

We need to build on what we know, what we already do well, in a balanced approach. Cooperative Learning as *one good tool* is great. Adopting it wholeheartedly as *the* great salvation of our nation's schools is foolishness, and certainly not what its proponents intend. The current Whole Language movement, though admirable in its goals, has similar dangers if embraced as an antidote to phonics and the teaching of the alphabet, rather than as an enhancement to limited, overly mechanistic means of language teaching/learning (MacGinitie, 1991).

TEACHING/LEARNING

You see that "teaching/learning" again. I believe that the two are not only inseparable, but they are meaningless when separated. We are making a continuous mistake when we separate the learning from the teaching, the learner from the teacher, and the teaching/learning from the curriculum. Arthur Koestler said, "Creative activity could be described as a type of learning process where teacher and pupil are locked in the same individual." What we have been doing more and more in recent years is relying on catchphrases such as "delivery of instruction" to substitute for teaching/learning. Does genuine knowledge come from UPS?

When we reduce the word and the concept of teacher (or teacher/ learner) to "instructor," we unnecessarily "clinicize" and subsequently dehumanize and diminish the role and the related attitude of and for the teacher. When we reduce the teaching/learning experience to "content coverage," we do the same thing. This leads to a demeaning of the experience and of the profession, often unwittingly. Such thoughtlessness at best, or insensitivity and poor pedagogy at worst, also keeps the student (or learner/teacher) in an unhealthy, passive, and decidedly less productive role (Eisner, 1985; Freire, 1957). Separating the behavior of the student (l/t) from the conditions of the teaching/learning environment is another thoughtless, yet often prevalent practice (Hilliard, 1991; Comer, in Moyers, 1989). We need to be far more thoughtful about what we are saying and what we are doing. Let's look in more depth at what we are doing in thousands of American schools.

SQUARE BODIES AND FAT HEADS

Glance in the door of the typical classroom. What do you see? The student desks are arranged in a large square, five across, six deep. They all face the front of the room, with all students looking toward the teacher, or into the backs of other students' heads. In the front of the room is the teacher desk and/or lectern, the place of the teacher. This is the *Fat Head* capping the *Square Body* (see Figure 1). This one shape is predominant in class after class, school after school, as if there were no other way to arrange twenty to thirty people in a room. The student desks are bad enough, small, confining, uncomfortable. This arrangement virtually guarantees that students remain in a passive, dependent mode while they are supposed to function "successfully." It is another remnant of the old factory model prevalent in our schools.

THE METASUBJECT

And what course is being taught in all of these Square Body/Fat Head boxes? Just one course. It is *The Metasubject*. The Metasubject includes science, math, foreign language, social studies, and English ("language arts" being a misnomer in this case). If it is a Square Body/Fat Head setup, with the teacher dominating, doing most of the talking, most of the questioning, with all discussion terminating at the teacher, and the students passively dependent, stuck in a "guess the right answer" mode, it is the Metasubject. This we call "terminal teaching," with the teacher functioning somewhat as a repository in a toxic waste dump (see Figure 2).

Now go away from there, to another wing in the building. Look for activity, listen for human and artificial sound, seek out variety of color, light, space, aesthetics. Find a place where the adult is one with the group, serving as mentor and coach, rather than as talk talk talker/teller (see Figure 3). Note that information flows in a variety of ways—to, through, behind, and around the teacher—in a "develop your own thoughtful question" mode. This is *The Other Subject*. The Other

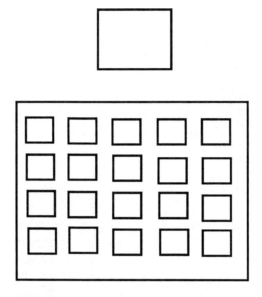

FIGURE 1. *Square Body/Fat Head Classroom.*

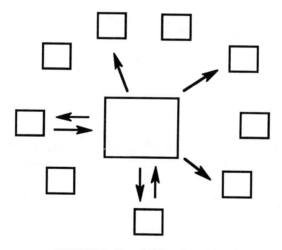

FIGURE 2. *Terminal Teaching Model.*

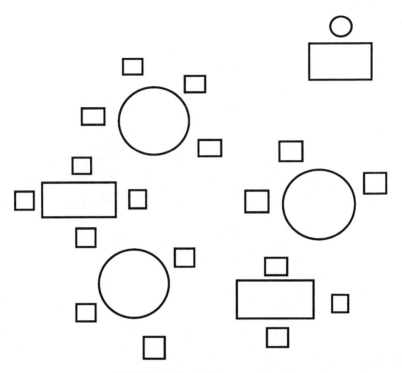

FIGURE 3. *Whole Classroom Gestalt.*

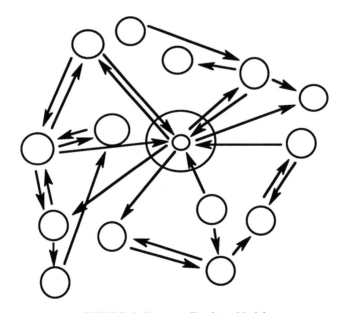

FIGURE 4. *Terminus Teaching Model.*

12

Subject may include art, performing music groups, athletics, home economics, technology shop, drama, computer lab, and student activities such as yearbook, newspaper, and government. Here the teacher engages in "terminus" teaching, functioning as a roundhouse in a locomotive switching yard (see Figure 4). Such a teacher facilitates and monitors the action, sometimes stopping all to introduce a new concept, or to more formally explore a current step in the process.

It isn't that the *courses* of The Metasubject are bad or wrong. It isn't that art and music are somehow better than history or literature. It is the means by which they are being taught; it is the "gestalt" or form of the environment that is so limiting, so detrimental to so many students, so antithetical to the way in which people most effectively learn new things, even to the very way in which the brain works.

JOY/RIGOR

The traditional dichotomy of joy and rigor is another issue that requires fresh and holistic thought. There is a prevalent myth that if a teaching/learning experience is too enjoyable it is somehow academically suspect. If it is "rigorous," or, better yet, painful, then it must have merit. This thinking is reminiscent of the bleaker side of the Protestant Work Ethic. It is the kind of thinking that leads well-meaning teachers in "good" schools to give two hours of homework to fourth graders, although there is no evidence to support the academic validity of such a practice, and it flies in the face of what we know about healthy childhood.

It is also a critical issue when a middle-level school is attempting transformation. The "rigorists" will oppose efforts to make the program more humane, more whole. They will see transescents on the playground at lunch and get anxious, wondering what is happening, fearful that the school is turning into a playschool. They will interpret comments made by seventh graders at dinner to the effect that, "We had fun in science today," to mean that all serious learning has been swept aside in the rush to "feel good."

An alternative myth generates a fear on the part of the "humanists," parents and teachers alike. Although far quieter in the typical public school community, they believe that homework stultifies creativity and leads to hatred of school and should never be given at all—especially if they have to help with it, or review it. A rounder view might be that homework as a tool to increase and extend learning can be quite productive in middle school—if assignments are thoughtful, whole, relevant to classroom experience, and generally no longer than an hour per night total. Homework can be highly effective in high school under the same conditions up to two plus hours per night. (U.S. Dept. of Education, 1989).

Now this is not meant to imply that if it is painful it is *necessarily bad*, or that if it is enjoyable it is *necessarily good*. That kind of thinking led an acquaintance of mine to drink large amounts of Scotch whenever he wished to write—because he wanted to be a writer and several of his favorite authors were alcoholics. Again we are emphasizing balance.

> Cursed be the dullard who destroys wonder.—*Alfred North Whitehead*

When do we fully and finally accept that the strongest teaching/ learning experiences are whole ones; that they contain elements of rigor, of joy, of doubt, of confidence, of seeking, of finding, of stimulation, of contentment, of excitement, of utter confusion—sometimes simultaneously? Is it not so that our favorite teachers (our best teachers), though not alike, were deep, varied, thoughtful, challenging, intriguing, unpredictable people who never let us get complacent, but always cared about us on a human level? They provided a "terminus" teaching/learning framework that was more whole, more rigorous, more engaging, more enjoyable, more passionate even, and ultimately more fulfilling than other classes and other teachers were. They provided balance, depth, and great emotional and intellectual care, even though at times that care could be very abstract.

What our best teachers provided was something that modern researchers on brain-based teaching/learning are strongly advocating. These scholars find ample evidence that cognitive, affective, and psychomotor experience is not disparate, discrete, nor easily compartmentalized. We have long been thinking that way in schools, however. Then, when we begin to recognize that knowing something about the brain's functioning might help us to improve school experience, we leap into the hemisphericity model—a right brain/left brain dichotomy that fit exactly into our preconceived, either/or thinking.

Actually we now know that, too, was simplistic. The brain localizes broad capacities, but only to a degree, and only in the absence of the corpus callosum, which connects the two halves. A whole brain acts like a whole brain, as a whole body acts like a whole body (Caine and Caine, 1991; Pearce, 1985). Both hemispheres are involved in all activities. Rather than a mechanistic machine with two distinct parts, the brain is a holographic phenomenon that deals with parts and wholes, and all aspects of reality simultaneously.

PROCESS/PRODUCT

One element of our favorite teachers' success was the fusion of process and product. Unlike in Square Body/Fat Head boxes, process and product are not separate in effective teaching/learning environments. Marshall McCluhan told us nearly three decades ago that "the medium is the message." His wonderful, ever-current book, *The Medium Is the Massage: An Inventory of Effects*, co-authored with Quentin Fiore, described the way the information age was transforming us. Yet their section on education depicted the obsolescence of the unstimulating "nineteenth century" schoolroom, with its factory assembly line approach to the gathering of "information that is scarce, but ordered and structured by fragmented, classified patterns, subjects, and schedules." They accurately predicted its demise as a valid system, its demise for not learning from the high-tech, high-stimulus world outside the schoolroom walls.

Strong teaching/learning environments do learn. They also grow and prosper in part because within them "process" and "product" are one process/product. This is true of the best Other Subject classes. Quality is expected and recognition of it is modelled and taught by a genuine teacher/learner. There is quality in the human interactions, and the concomitant production reflects that quality. The school then is not separate from learning, it is not separate from life. Students as learners/ teachers are encouraged to engage in the process/product, are involved in decisions relating to that engagement, and are provided with real tools, mental, social, and physical, to fashion something special (Sternberg and Lubart, 1991).

The classroom is a rich, colorful, diverse environment full of fine student displays. The windows open to the world, people move purposefully, technology is an ally, the community is included in the process/product, and the learners/teachers work independently and together on intellectually artistic projects of high interest, sustained commitment, and great challenge. The teacher/learner is their coach and mentor. That mentor is less concerned with the limiting "which" and "what"—even while becoming expert in the "how" and the "where" of accessing information, and in the "why" and the "us" of quality teaching/learning.

3

BEGINNING STUDENT MORALE PROGRAMS, ENDING STUDENT DISCIPLINE PROBLEMS

> *Education is the guidance of the individual towards*
> *a comprehension of the art of life.*
> *—ALFRED NORTH WHITEHEAD*

THE ANALOGY OF THE DOORWAY

Every day at 11:56 A.M. hundreds of seventh graders hit the main corridor doorway to the cafeteria. Invariably they bump and jostle one another. The boys especially love the excuse to bang into someone else. Although the pushing is basically good-natured, often someone will go too far, and the other may feel called to retaliate. A push becomes an elbow becomes a fist—suddenly a fight breaks out. Students watch in fascination or horror until the assailants are separated by the feverish assistant principal. He drags them away to his office, still kicking and screaming.

Once there behind closed doors the interrogation begins. Witnesses will have to be rounded up as well. Because it is the first fight for one and the third for the other, different consequences will result. Regulations must be followed, forms filled out in detail, parents contacted. If there is a suspension, classwork will have to be obtained from teachers, perhaps a test will need to be made up as well. If there is injury, the nurse must be involved. The need for a counselor is quite possible.

What results from this simple altercation is: (1) a violent spectacle in a central area witnessed by dozens of students and staff, and perhaps visitors; (2) resulting profanity and defiance directed at the assistant principal; (3) a long procedure determining culpability; (4) negative contacts with at least two homes; (5) taking of up to an hour, or more, of the valuable time of the assistant principal; (6) taking the time of the nurse, possibly one or more counselors, and secretarial time as well; (7) taking the time of someone to transport the suspended student home when parents cannot; (8) persistent bad feelings on the part of the combatants, witnesses, parents, et al.; and (9) numerous other subtle and not so subtle ramifications in the life of the school.

What should be done here? Some obvious suggestions might be

- Make students walk more slowly in the halls.
- Banish fighters from the lunchroom for two weeks.
- Post clear hall rules for everybody.
- Establish a tighter school discipline code.
- Begin a Conflict Resolution program.
- Do more affective education training.
- Assign more staff to hall duty.
- Expect that administrators become more "visible."
- Set up Advisories so kids could have better relationships.
- Bring parents in for STEP training.

Some of these are sounder than others and any one of them might provide some short-term relief. Several could be valid interventions in their own right. But there is a simpler, sounder, easier solution than any of these: *widen the doorway.*

MORALE RATHER THAN DISCIPLINE

The amount and intensity of student discipline problems are reflective of the level of student morale in the building. When morale is high, discipline problems are low and vice versa. Actions that focus on symptoms rather than causes are generally far less effective than a whole, person-centered approach. (We say "person-centered" because a student-centered approach that functions at the expense of the teachers is just as bad for a school as a teacher-centered approach at the expense of the students.) Therefore, instituting a Conflict Resolution program while classroom teachers are still failing dozens of students who already have low self-esteem is probably not going to do it.

A transformed school does not lack structure. What distinguishes it from a dysfunctional school are the dimensions and the quality of its structure.

STUDENT RECOGNITION

You have heard that, "We value what we can measure." Why save the joy and recognition for the end of the year, for the "good" kids who win everything, for one long assembly that may become boring to many of the kids? Why use grades as the carrots and sticks, reducing education to a numbers game, making grades *the* end-product rather than *a* by-product of learning? (Please see Chapter 9.) A strong student recognition program is a proven, powerfully proactive element of any transformation process.

Three Grand Assemblies

At our school we held three awards assemblies for each grade every three months. In those assemblies we celebrated our school slogan: "Learning, Caring, Growing, Sharing," by giving awards to four different students in each of four categories: Effort (I Learn Award), Citizenship (I Care Award), Improvement (I Grow Award), and Friendship (I Share Award). Each assembly was about twenty minutes long. Student leaders read a statement about the significance of each award, called up the kids, and I shook the hand of each student and presented them with handsome certificates. Parents and friends were invited to the assembly and a reception for the award winners and their families was held right after the ceremony. Later, the kids from all three grades would go to Pizza Hut for lunch with staff members.

Students could win in two categories per year, but no more than two. This process enabled us to give as many as 120 different awards of this type annually to a student body of 670 kids. It was special, but still within the reach of virtually every student during his or her tenure at the school. By awarding them for such varieties of behavior (all quite important in a school) we broadened the possibility still more.

The feeling I would have standing on the stage seeing kids come up—kids of every background and type, kids who were model students coming up there with kids who had never won anything in their lives and had had no expectation of winning anything prior to coming to that school—was phenomenal. And it did not take long for that process to become an institution, something that even "very cool" middle-level kids came to anticipate and cherish.

The Wonderful Box

We set up a Wonderful Box in the office. Anybody at any time could place a paper with the name and accomplishments of someone else in the school (adult and/or student) in that box. Within a day or two a display board in the main corridor would show that recognition. The only problem with it was that our EMR class often had the assignment of updating the information—and their spelling was not the best.

Letter of Commendation

Too often the only official communication from school direct to the individual home is a report card, or a discipline letter. We designed a Letter of Commendation that listed a score of behaviors and attitudes we found valuable. All staff had to do was write the student's name at the top, circle any appropriate items and sign it. It was deliberately easy for us, and it was special for the student and parent. Any student at any time might receive such a letter from a teacher, counselor, or administrator. We sent hundreds each year and they were appreciated tremendously.

(Years ago I sent such a letter to a high school sophomore student of mine who had a sad and troubled history, but who was making great progress in my class. A bit later he got into a scrape with a particularly provocative kid and pulled a knife on him, but did not use it. At his expulsion hearing his grandmother, who was his one available relative, produced the letter of commendation as her grandson's only tangible means of defense. As a result of the letter and a subsequent discussion between the superintendent and me, the young man was not expelled. He went on to star on the varsity basketball team and graduate with his class. We are friends to this day.)

One thing to consider with this letter is whether to formalize it, or leave the format to an individual teacher's discretion. Some teachers never cared for the formality of our letter, preferring to create their own means of recognition.

Students on Display

One night each May we hosted a spectacular student performance event in which we celebrated the achievements of our students in the fine arts, practical arts, technology, science and social studies fair projects, etc. In a three-ring circus type format we held a host of student performances, demonstrations, plays, videos, speeches, and more. We had food and festivity and a thousand or more visitors to the school.

This is an event that requires a great deal of teacher preparation time. Holding it at the end of the year with all the other things going on may prove difficult for some staff members. Generally our staff felt that the May timing was optimal, although there were a few who saw it as an imposition.

Awards Night

We always concluded our year with a wonderful, traditional awards ceremony as well. We honored our strongest scholars, the winners of various regional and state competitions, students of the year in various teams, President's Academic Fitness Award recipients, and so on. We also created a new award known as "The Right Stuff Award" and presented it to four outstanding eighth graders. Our criterion was that these were terrific kids, well-rounded, but not necessarily the "best" at any one thing. They were solid, neat, with-it kids who were often amazed that they had won. Their parents were so proud.

Altogether we would give as many as 100 awards on this special night. We would have student speeches of intensity and thought, student musical interludes, and a high level of decorum and presentation throughout, without it ever getting boring. What a fine way to end a year.

This too takes a great deal of effort on the part of many staff. The more that administrators and secretaries can do directly, the better. Efforts of this magnitude will come forth more easily as the transformation progresses, and as people feel more and more hooked into it all, and become less inclined to measure their contributions.

MORALE IMPROVEMENT SYSTEMS

A foolish consistency is the hobgoblin of little minds.
— *Ralph Waldo Emerson*

Two School Rules

Get rid of your forty-seven-page student handbook. Get rid of your lists of rules and regulations, lists of "can'ts" and "don'ts." We replaced our forty-seven-page student handbook with a glossy student folder.

All essential procedures were printed on that folder, given to each student the first day of school and whenever they asked for one. The dominant theme becomes "student self-discipline." The tone of the folder, including the ubiquitous message from the principal, should be thoroughly positive and mature. Rather than defining bad behavior and its punishments, the folder describes appropriate behavior and its benefits.

There are only two specific rules that need to be mentioned in the folder, and those rules should also be posted in every classroom and in the assistant principal's office: *Respect People, Respect Property.* These are two terrific, all-inclusive rules. Virtually every concern falls under one category or the other, especially when you remind students that *self-respect* belongs under Respect People.

Flexible Procedures

Don't box yourself in on punishments (see Emerson above). Lists of procedures and "steps" are wonderfully handy, especially for the less imaginative, less assertive teacher or administrator. But they will tie your hands. They will lead to endless issues of fairness, of interpretation, of comparison, of implementation, of modification. You are much better with fluid thinking and flexible action. Students need to know there are consequences for poor choices. They also need to know that there is a bottom line – that they cannot misbehave endlessly with no serious repercussions. They do not need to know much more than that.

As anyone familiar with "doing discipline" will tell you, it is infinitely complex, and every case is a little bit different. Just as courts have leeway in their sentencing procedures, so should schools have leeway in their "consequencing" procedures. The most important thing is that there is always a consequence – even if it is just a talk with the teacher in the hall. The Discipline Referral Form in the Appendix details a long list of appropriate teacher and administrator responses to student misbehavior.

Change Behavior, Don't Simply Punish It

The goal here is to change the behavior to prevent recurrence. Just looking at the list and assigning the punishment will not accomplish that in many cases. You have rule 42.4, 6C: ANYONE CURSING A

STAFF MEMBER WILL BE SUSPENDED FOR TWO DAYS. How do you respond "fairly" when (1) the valedictorian, having the worst day of his life, mutters under his breath to Ms. Tinkerton, "Give me a damn break"; or (2) the nastiest dude in the eighth grade chooses a full school assembly as his place to shout, "Hey, _____ you! You dumb _____er!" to the principal? And this is the fifth time that he has said it. I am not sure that suspension is going to have the desired effect in either case, but I sure don't like to be boxed in on my response—not with the student, the teacher, or the parents.

Over time, through a variety of methods, most students come to see the value in making sounder choices, especially when they *will definitely benefit* from them. Students do not like to be in trouble. They often do like attention, however, and if they are not getting it positively, they will get it negatively.

Listen to Their Stories

As one who has dealt with a full range of students and made most of the mistakes possible in this terribly difficult area, I can say that some methods work better than others. I have shouted and whispered to them, laughed, joked, and cried with them, hugged and nearly choked kids.

My first month as principal ended in a physical confrontation in the corridor with a drugged and violent high school student who refused to stop coming into our school and harassing our students and teachers. That appeared to be the appropriate response at the time—it certainly enabled me to get better control of the situation. But I am not at all sure if that is really ever the best way in the long term with any kid, or any situation. I have had greater success and felt better during and afterward through taking a higher road.

Generally speaking, I would say do not argue, struggle with, or attempt to overpower the disruptive, strong-willed, needy student. Find fifteen minutes and listen to her/his story. It will be the most productive fifteen minutes you can spend. It will be far more productive than the fifteen one- to thirty-minute episodes resulting from your failure to "connect" with that young person—for the strong-willed, needy kid will get you one way or the other. So you can choose for it to be a much more positive form of attention through this simple technique.

Find a quiet, private place. Your classroom or office at lunch time, or after class, is fine, but preferably not after some misbehavior by the student. Ask a few non-threatening, but leading, questions about what is really on the kid's mind. Then give that kid your full attention and just listen. You will be amazed. You might also end up in tears.

The Story of Laura Dean

My first year as principal there was a sixteen-year-old eighth grader whom we will call Laura Dean. She was big, she was tough, and she was as volatile as a hand grenade nine seconds after pin-pulling. She normally dressed in black, with short skirt, too much dark eye shadow, and pointed black boots. Many teachers disliked Laura, and she was less than fond of them. If she wanted something from a student, she took it. The baddest boys didn't mess with Laura — she'd tear their eyes out in a heartbeat. After a couple of weeks of letting the assistant principal try to deal with the frequent Laura-storms, I needed to get involved. The moment I met with her privately the first time, I realized that this was a person of immense power, and immense pain.

When I listened to her story, I felt my own heart tremble, and I did end up in tears. At the age of seven, in a horrible family row, Laura tried desperately to prevent her drunken father from shooting her screaming mother. She failed. Then he turned the gun on himself and blew his head off in front of Laura and her little brother and sister. Despite a wound in the chest, her mother survived. She never recovered emotionally, however, and abandoned the children for Florida shortly afterward.

After separation from her siblings and several years with various foster parents, Laura tracked down her mom and her mom's boyfriend. At the age of twelve Laura moved in with them and in the process became the first girl to play interscholastic football for a boys' team in the state of Florida. She was briefly featured on a national news spot. Despite great frustration, physical pain, and verbal abuse, Laura played out the season as a defensive end.

That was her only year at that school. Her mom left her for the second time and Laura turned north to seek her brother and sister once more. Now, by the age of thirteen, she had known many men, many drugs, and unimaginable heartbreak.

Judged unfit to live with her siblings, she was only allowed to visit when she could manage — a couple of times a year at best. At the time of our first talk she was living with an abusive aunt, sharing her bed with a thirty-year-old man, and trying desperately to keep cigarettes and soda as her only active addictions. She told me that she could not sleep deeply—ever. Whenever she tried, she was beset with the terrible nightmare visions of that violent scene.

What I learned was not how awful Laura was, but rather how incredibly *together* she was considering her situation—present and past. I came to respect, admire, and love her. I soon discovered that none of her teachers knew her full story, or the extent of the trauma she endured. From the time of that first visit, Laura and I never had a personal clash—although she was in continual trouble through the rest of the school year, as we held her by a thread. In fact when she did "go off" I could calm her down with a touch on her forearm, and the simple human understanding that we had.

So a teacher or administrator takes a risk when she/he listens to such a student, such a story. You will hear about deprivation, intense loneliness, fear, anger, abandonment, maybe abuse. It is a truism that every kid who has serious trouble in school has trouble outside of school. Though you may not be trained as a counselor, you do know much about communicating and you can feel comfortable that if you trust your instincts and allow your humanity to come forth, something fine will occur.

You Won't Get Jammed Again

Then, when you have listened, you can share. Telling students about your own past, your difficulties, your own struggle to fulfill your dreams is so powerful. It makes you real to the student, just as hearing that young person makes her/him real to you. Generally once you submit to this process that student will never "jam" you again—just as hard-as-nails Laura never jammed me again. You won't solve the larger problems, but you will greatly improve your part in it, your relationship. That is the most important element for you anyway—and the only one you *can* do much about. Once your relationship with that kid in class, or in the halls, is no longer problematical, it allows for all manner of improvement in other realms to occur. It is good for you, too, for as Lincoln said, "To ease another's heartache is to forget one's own."

If we can not find time for their stories—the least we can do is read their folders. It is hard to believe, but I have dealt with more than one teacher over the years who had the time to complain incessantly about a student's behavior in class, yet never found ten minutes to walk to guidance and read that kid's folder, uncover something essential about that kid's problems, and touch that kid's past in a simple attempt at improving that kid's present.

For every one of these, however, I have known at least another who would do anything possible to make that student's experience more positive, more whole. Most educators begin as idealists, after all. It is the matter of remaining so that is our purpose here.

4

ORGANIZE AWAY PROBLEMS

*The central problem with the rationalist
view of organizing people is that
people are not very rational.*
—TOM PETERS AND ROBERT WATERMAN

ELIMINATE BELLS

We had all of the typical middle level hall and cafeteria problems until we implemented several changes and thus "organized them away."

Eliminate bells. Have a schedule, but no bells. Like college. Like life. It works fine. Stop "fire-alarming" the school ten or more times per day, and everyone will slow down. Teachers end classes, not bells, and they like that. Students are excellent at reminding teachers when it is time, so they are not let out late by mistake. However, if a teacher needs time to finish something (and in a teaming, block schedule, the teacher knows where the kids are going next—and may be getting that other teacher's whole class anyway), a student can be sent to alert the next teacher that the kids will be a few minutes late and it isn't a problem.

You will also no longer have kids piling up at water fountains waiting for the bell to ring—and then running to class. If kids are a few seconds late, no big deal. If they are chronically late, normal procedures for that offense can be enacted. We had far *fewer* tardies to class without bells than with them. I was nominated for a No-Bell Prize, but never received a nickel for it.

UNPLUG THE P.A. SYSTEM

Just do it! Again, it isn't used in the real world and life goes on quite nicely. The only problem you will have is finding a new way to meet the power needs of your secretary. If schools are truly purposeful educa-

27

tional organizations we cannot allow every single person to be blasted with that stupid P.A. every day. It is a horribly disruptive, unproductive device that is demeaning to everyone in the building, child or adult. It is amazing that they are still being used indiscriminately in so many schools.

I was once in a districtwide in-service in a high school in which the secretary on the P.A. interrupted 400 staff members in various and productive meetings to ask whose parking lights were on. I was at an elementary school, in a meeting with administrators, and the secretary informed the entire school population (including children six years old) over the P.A. that "There has been a plane crash. Senator Smith has been killed and so were two elementary students."

The sharing of such sensitive and disturbing information in this manner with anyone, let alone little kids who had no idea who/what/where is mind-boggling. (The accident occurred fifteen miles away and did not involve anyone from the district.) It is also directly opposed to what we know about sharing just such information. What I found even more intriguing was that no one in my group, which included the school principal, even raised an eyebrow!

There is no excuse for the silly, obsolete P.A. Beepers take care of calling custodians, reading written announcements each day in homeroom takes care of general information sharing, and either calling individuals on phones, finding them (yes, walking!), or taking a message for them takes care of other forms of personal communication. The P.A. serves as another excuse to be inefficient and needlessly disruptive. Every time it is used it sends a message that what you are doing is less important than what it is doing. Another simple solution: pull the plug.

STAGGER RELEASE TIMES

Stagger the schedule and release times for all students. By putting each grade on a five-minute stagger, hall crowding is cut by two-thirds. Younger students go to the buses first and unhassled. By further staggering the release of individual teams to the cafeteria, eliminate lunch lines, and kids can get their food as they arrive. Four self-service lines (two cashiers) also expedite cafeteria efficiency and cut down on waste as kids individualize their own portions.

SANE-ITIZE THE CAFETERIA

Don't keep kids in the cafeteria after they are done eating. You are just "beggin' for a peggin' " if you do. We sent them out after twenty-five minutes to the forum area across the hall (any large open space is fine) where they had approximately fifteen minutes to hang out, talk, socialize in an acceptable manner. If they are too rambunctious standing up, have them sit down in groups with their friends. Using exterior spaces and/or the gymnasium are additional options. If your students are generally responsible, some form of an "open campus" will work well.

By using separate doors we had it down to where a new grade of kids was coming onto the lunch lines before the others even left the cafeteria. When kids know they won't have to wait long in line, they also stop running.

By assigning the same staff every day to monitor the same kids in both the cafeteria and the forum afterwards (or before, depending on which grade) you maintain continuity of expectations and of behavior. This way a few teachers have lunch duty, and they may even have it in place of a fifth teaching assignment. Under such a plan most teachers avoid "the hated lunch duty" altogether.

Encourage staff to eat in the cafeteria with students. Have days when Advisories eat lunch together with their Teacher Advisor. Maintain regular, positive interaction between supervisory staff and students.

Examine the food content to make sure that it is in keeping with your school goals. Our goals were centered on humane development of the whole child, including the physical. (More on goals in Chapter 11.) When we eliminated most of the junk food previously available, put in a salad bar, and got rid of chocolate milk and soda machines, we also noticed an increase in afternoon productivity of our students, and the end to the sugar-fits and subsequent low-sugar energy crash we had grown accustomed to.

Through a holistic look at your cafeteria experience, it can go from being the worst part of the school day to becoming a truly enjoyable, healthy, and trouble-free one.

ABOLISH LEPER COLONIES

Another thing we took a long look at was the existence of Leper Colonies. Leper Colonies are groupings of student outcasts, under-achievers, and misfits in the school. To set them up as part of the program is to guarantee low self-esteem in those quarantined students. This practice also engenders a biased, judgemental, stigmatizing view of others in a large sector of the student body and of the staff.

Examples of Leper Colonies are:

- large remedial classes
- low-level tracked classes in any subject
- detention halls
- vocational education classes
- in-school suspension pits
- special education classes comprised of isolated teachers and students in remote or undesirable spaces
- self-contained special education classes where students and teacher rarely interact with the rest of the school populace
- elective classes in which only low-achieving students enroll
- a section of the cafeteria where only black tee-shirt kids sit sullenly

A well-intentioned, quasi-innovative, but equally misguided Leper Colony is the Alternative Program that takes twenty to forty at-risk kids and puts them all together in a Core curricular setting for a large part or all of the day.

A Leper Colony is any environment intentionally filled with more than five or so academic losers. It is any room or program that is easily identifiable just by seeing all the miserable kids within it (or all the minority kids, or all the blue jean jackets).

Sometimes some of these programs may be partially successful, especially if there are other positive experiences for the "lepers" during the remainder of the day, or if there is a wonderful, pied piper for a teacher. Any program that is personality-dependent is also highly vulnerable should that teacher leave—and just those types of teachers often do! The point is that there are better ways of dealing with your at-risk kids than by establishing Leper Colonies—much better ways.

We had all of these Leper Colonies when I started as principal: all but an Alternative Program, which the high school generously provided for us. We also had all of the problems detailed in the introduction. After my first two years we had no Leper Colonies. And we also had dramatically lower problem rates—and no dropouts, *zero* in our third year.

By instituting wholesale attitudinal change along with basic programmatical change we created a new set of beliefs, expectations, and behaviors in our students and in our staff. We

- developed a Learning Lab to replace remedial classes, eliminated vocational classes, modified grouping and eliminated tracking (see Chapters 9 and 10)
- incorporated all of our learning-disabled (LD) students, teachers, and classrooms right into our teaming structure, mixed our educable mentally retarded (EMR) into typical student-teacher advisory groups, into elective classes, and into many other school activities, and mainstreamed all but a very few emotionally disabled (ED) students who had previously been self-contained (see Chapters 6 and 7)
- instituted a dress code wherein vile and offensive tee-shirts, and torn or suggestive clothing were no longer considered acceptable school attire (although students became freer in other, more healthy ways to express themselves, and so it never became a big issue)
- eliminated detention and replaced the in-school suspension "dungeon" with an Alternative Learning Center (see below)

DETENTION

This may have an even easier solution than turning off the bells or pulling the P.A. plug. Get rid of it. Eliminate detention as an alternative for teachers. As long as there are other sound alternatives (and we provide quite a few herein) this tired old mess will not be missed. All the concomitant problems of record-keeping, upset kids, upset parents, principals chasing everybody around, kids cutting detention, and the ultimate issue—which is that detention usually does not solve, but only postpones, a real solution of the basic student-teacher problem—will not be missed either.

CARE COMMITTEE

We did not like calling our at-risk kids by that pejorative name. So we formed the acronym CARE for "Children At Risk in Education." (Since then we have seen other versions of this acronym used elsewhere and think that's great.) Then we developed a comprehensive form that we used school systemwide to identify and monitor our CARE kids. We knew who they were before they came to us from the elementary schools, and we kept updated records on all of them throughout their stay with us. We then forwarded such a form with them to the high school upon their leaving us—if they were still on the CARE list.

Our CARE Committee had a representative from each teaching team, a guidance counselor, the district at-risk coordinator, and our assistant principal serving as chairperson. Meeting every two weeks, they consistently reviewed and upgraded the status of every member of the fluid CARE list. We kept a "Top 10" of those most in need of care—the list consisting either of those most likely to cause severe problems, or those most likely to drop out (see Appendix). Those are generally two very different types of kids. We also had a *Student Alert Form* (see Appendix) that was circulated to all appropriate staff members when any student, though most often a CARE student, was in a special condition of stress. Such extreme stress might involve a traumatic event outside of school, expression of suicidal tendencies, observed substance abuse, or something equally severe.

By (1) identifying CARE students, (2) monitoring their progress, (3) developing intervention strategies, and (4) reevaluating them frequently we were able to make definitive progress in enabling those students to become substantially more successful in school. In concert with all the other programs in place, such success was clearly demonstrated by a significant reduction of the CARE list over time. In our third year it went from a September total of 77 to a June total of 43, despite the addition of several students to the list during the year.

Through the CARE Committee's work in concert with our Whole School approach, we enabled dozens of students to experience full success in school for the first time. In many instances the turnaround was as dramatic as that of students who got mostly F's in their previous schools making our A-B Honor Roll, or that of a former delinquent home resident, sent there for violent and sexual acts, who became a leader in his only year with us, starter on the eighth grade football and basketball teams, and was not suspended a single day in the year (though he had a few "brushes!").

ALC: THE ALTERNATIVE LEARNING CENTER

ALC works on several levels simultaneously. It can be used as an in-school suspension vehicle (although with several modifications), as a time-out, short-term place; as an assigned study time; as a voluntary, student-initiated study time; or even as a voluntary "get my head together" time-out place.

If it is run thoughtfully, an Alternative Learning Center will provide a tremendous benefit. The first requirement is a full-time person to staff it and assume responsibility for it. Our plan included a teacher with counseling certification to coordinate the program and a part-time assistant teacher to cover for him when he was on break, had planning, or another teaching assignment. In our equivalent of a seven-period day the ALC coordinator spent four periods in the room, and his assistant spent three each day. He took the first three periods and the last one. This maintained continuity, consistency, and control for students who were assigned a full day or longer. It also ensured that assigned students got off to an appropriate start each morning.

Several other elements are important also. The space should be a *positive* one—not a "dungeon." It should be bright, attractive, full of positive images, a few upbeat slogans perhaps, and good furniture. We used our ALC as an advisory space also and the ALC coordinator and his group met there during daily homeroom/advisory time. This "mainstreamed" the space and the teacher, further "de-leperizing" both. The ability of the ALC coordinator as a calming, firm influence, a tutor, and a counselor is also key. There should be no more than eight to ten students in the room at any one time.

ALC is not a place in which kids will want to spend long amounts of time because it is not ordinary and no socializing is allowed. A student in all day would miss lunch with his peers also, eating after the last lunch shift. It is not a hateful place, however. It is a place to cool out and get things together again before returning to the normal life of the school. There is a caring, competent adult there to assist the student academically and psychoemotionally.

ALC is perhaps most effectively utilized when students who are assigned there (and only administrators assign students to ALC directly through the ALC coordinator) have a minimum sentence, not a maximum. Then a student is sent to ALC for one day *but* may be released at lunch if he/she does "a good job" while in ALC. A student is sent for three days, which can commute to a day and a half for good behavior, and so on. This "working your way out early" becomes a powerful incentive for students to comply with the ALC code. That code is essentially the school code: *Respect People, Respect Property.* Expectations for behavior are clear and consistent, mirroring the two school rules, while providing specific direction for working most productively. This is an excellent way to empower students, to help them assume responsibility for both their unacceptable and their improved behavior, and thereby to help meet the goal of changing behavior rather than simply punishing it.

Most of the time (95%) students will work their way out early if enabled to do so. This also makes the whole environment in ALC much more palatable and calm for all. When you assign absolute sentences, students are more likely to rebel (especially if they feel the punishment is unfair anyway—which they often originally do) and act out (knowing that they have to stay that long anyway).

What often results *if* (1) there is no way to get out early, (2) it is too grim, stark, and punitive, or (3) the coordinator is cold and uncaring (or lax and inattentive) *is* (1) longer sentences for misbehaving reprobates, (2) worse behavior, since students know they cannot maintain for, say, five days in the tank, and then (3) no alternative but out-of-school suspension for misbehaving in ALC. The eventual punishment then no longer fits the original crime at all. This will cause great friction with kids and great mistrust with certain parents who tend to side with their children on such issues.

After the ALC program was fully established, it was not uncommon for a student to ask a staff member if she/he could go to ALC for a time to catch up on work, to calm down after something traumatic at home, or to simply get a change of pace from the intensity of normal school routine. When that occurs, you know that ALC is fulfilling a need at many levels. And to paraphrase Eldridge Cleaver, that philosopher/incarcerate who could probably relate to ALC as well as anyone, it then has "become part of the solution, rather than part of the problem" in the transformation of your school.

5

QUALITY: THE SCHOOL AS A HUMANE BUSINESS

There is nothing so secular
that it cannot be sacred.
— MADELEINE L'ENGLE

SPACES

Here is another opportunity for us to think in wholes, rather than dichotomies. Often I have noticed that educators feel one of two ways: *either* the school is people-centered, pleasant, and sloppy, *or* it is well-organized, cold, and inhumane, "like a business." This is the classic process *versus* product dichotomy. It is unnecessary and unreal. The best businesses, like the best schools, are able to function efficiently *and* effectively. They are both functional and humane.

THE POWER OF APPEARANCES

What is the typical school entrance like? It will have a plastic sticker on the entrance door directing visitors to the main office, which is probably within feet of that door. It will be tiled and the tiles will probably be a bit worn, dated, and dulled. There may be notes and memos stuck to some wall, bulletin board, or window in a hodgepodge pattern. There may or may not be a direction box, a sign of greeting, a few plants, a poster, or a print. It will most likely be somewhat empty, cool, and even austere. The higher the school level, the grimmer the entrance. From this we might assume that only younger children, their parents, and teachers care about ambience.

I have entered a high school where the first thing one sees is a faded, unframed anti-drug poster depicting a drug addict sticking a needle in his arm. One windy day I visited a middle school and there were whirlwinds of trash and paper spinning all over the front grounds. At the entrance to another high school I know the only sign is one cautioning against drinking and driving: "Don't Drink and Drive High School."

What is the typical school main office like? It will have a long, high counter, centrally located. It will have secretaries' desks about. Those desks will have varied amounts of clutter depending on each secretary's style. There will be a bulletin board or two with announcements pinned all over them. Many of those announcements will be out of date. There will be a large, loud, and ugly copying machine. There will be a bank of teacher mailboxes. There will be a line of chairs for visitors. There will be a coffee maker with acrid black jet fuel simmering in its base, and some stained mugs hanging on pegs. There may be posters or prints—they may be attractive and new, probably not. There may be plants—they may be healthy and profuse, probably not.

In one state's model middle school I could barely wedge my way into the main office. There were students in two of the three (non-matching) chairs waiting to go home sick; the cakes and cookies on the dominant front counter were attracting sweet-minded, pleasant (though somewhat large-waisted) staff; secretaries and administrators bustled past through a space comfortably wide enough for one body; teachers piled in to get their mail from the stuffed little boxes; and other students in black Mega-Death tee-shirts went through that same space to be disciplined.

Winston Churchill said, "Man shapes the buildings, and thereafter the buildings shape man." An entrance to a building makes a statement, as does a main office. These are the first places staff see each day. These are often the only places many visitors see. They should be exceptional spaces, designed for function, for aesthetics, and for people. They should be designed carefully, tastefully, thoughtfully.

USING OFFICE SPACE PROFESSIONALLY

One should feel stimulated, welcomed, and engaged when one enters any building, especially a school full of vibrant young people. Get rid of the turn-off signs, the drug and alcohol awareness slogans, the cigarette butts on the steps. Get rid of the tired trophy cases and the tacky computer-printed signs. Put large, healthy plants around, great mirrors, beautiful prints, attractive modern furniture, one powerful slogan, and your finest student work. Make that lobby as elegant as a corporation, as warm as a fine home.

Do the same thing in the main office. Get rid of the giant counter. It serves as an unnecessary barricade with people. It accumulates paper and clutter like a huge suction device. Move the noisy, ugly copier. Get rid of the bulletin boards, with their mess. No one reads them there anyway. Replace them with attractively displayed school goals, framed posters and prints, and nothing. Get desks out of the main thoroughfare, keeping only reception stations out there, and spotless ones at that. Replace rotty old carpets and drapes. And always remember the motto of the now-defunct Chaskawaski Paint Corps: "It's amazing what a fresh coat of paint will do!"

Put in simple, tasteful furniture, and enough of it. Offer school brochures and professional journals instead of old notices and *People* magazine. Assign different functions to different spaces.

Look at your spaces in a fresh way and you will see that they can be used differently, more effectively, and probably without a whole lot of cost or renovation. Just as purchasing posters, plants, and decent furniture will not be a high ticket item, so will organizing spaces optimally prove to be more efficient—and wonderfully effective socially and professionally.

Spread out your functions. There should never be an upset student waiting to see the assistant principal anywhere near the main adult visitor space. There should be walls or at least visual barriers between visitor space and the teacher workplace or mail spaces also. This might sound obvious, but how do you do it in *your* school? Circular traffic patterns can be established. Glass block is wonderful for redefining office spaces. Put guidance somewhere else. Put the bookkeeper, the copier, and the coffee machine somewhere else. Be creative, be thoughtful, be professional. As Will Rogers said, "You only have one chance to make a first impression."

THE PROFESSIONALIZATION OF TEACHING

Attitude

Earlier we talked about attitude. Its value cannot be overstated. A shared feeling, esprit de corps, synergy, common commitment— whatever you want to call it—is essential if growth/improvement (G/I) is to occur and to last. Great attitude can be strengthened, developed, encouraged, brought in, perfected, or destroyed based on the practices and systems of a program.

The key people cannot compromise on the attitude they are seeking. They must model it as well. It is an attitude of *kaizen*, the "constant improvement" spoken of earlier. It is an attitude of risk-taking and encouragement of mistakes. Yes, encouragement. No mistakes means no risks means no G/I. It is an attitude of joyous intensity, of controlled looseness, of serious spontaneity, of organized chaos.

The central tenets of this attitude are that

- Teaching is a wonderful, noble, and essential calling.
- This organization is people-centered.
- We all do our best always.
- We are sensitive and thoughtful about everything we do.
- All children can learn, damn it!

The Seven-Word Teacher Handbook

We spoke earlier of replacing the forty-seven-page student handbook with a simple folder. Tom Peters tells us in *Thriving on Chaos* that the highly successful retailer, Nordstrom, replaced its employee manual with a sentence of seven words: *Use your best judgement at all times.* Wow. What that does for a staff! How freeing! We liked it so much we adopted it as our own "unofficial" teacher handbook. We were so busy with our transformation process that we never got around to replacing our cumbersome forty-seven-page teacher handbook. Finally we realized that it wasn't worth replacing. We knew what we were doing, we had synergistic thinking all over the place, and the majority of people simply didn't want or need a handbook.

Staff Building

It is important to take appropriate time with those people who do need more direction, more regulation as well. It takes time to wean organizationally-dependent people, to enable them to become more proactive, more confident, more team-oriented even as they become more effectively autonomous. Much care should be given to hiring; induction; placement of teachers in grade levels, subjects, and teams; training and retraining, etc.

Of these, *hiring* is easily the most important. If you want an exceptional school, never hire anyone who isn't already clearly exceptional. Those are the people you do not want to let get out of the interview room after you meet them. Every time someone new is hired, especially if it is a replacement for someone leaving, you have the opportunity, to "replace a number nine hitter with a number four hitter." Think about what that one change does to a lineup. The relative strength of everyone in the building is upgraded when that is done. When you settle for someone who is less than exceptional, you simply haven't looked hard enough, offered enough, or spent time enough. The best opportunity you have for "inside-out" transformation is lost.

It is a sad commentary on education that many school systems refuse to pay for all or part of someone's service in a previous position in another district. This nickel-dime approach to hiring is so counterproductive. I would argue that the most valuable staff member to obtain is generally the one who is a "young veteran," someone who is not just starting out but is still relatively youthful and vital. Talented people with three to ten years' experience are excellent additions to an older, tiring staff. If we will not place them in the appropriate place on the scale, will not consider their experience as economically valuable, why should they take the position? The best usually will not!

Constant teacher involvement and feedback is part of such processes when they are successful. Teachers should always be part of the interviewing process for any new staff. Teachers should be continually polled as to their preference for assignments, in-service topics, team placement, and leadership. Generally, staff will be moving in similar directions, thinking in similar ways, once the G/I momentum is established. Teachers must develop their own goals, sometimes with the assistance of a team leader or administrator. It is terribly unprofessional and counterproductive to simply hand them down their goals. The same is true of school and districtwide goals. Every member of the organization must be part of the process if the goals are to be valid and have impact (more on Goals in Chapter 11).

Eliminating "Role-Freeze"

We live in a new world of generalization and versatility. The more specialized and limited the job, the more likely it is to be replaced by a mechanical/electronic device or system. Strong middle-level schools need flexible, adaptable, multi-faceted staff willing and able to do much more than one thing. A typical middle-level teacher should be able to teach in at least two subject areas, run an advisory group, sponsor something, serve as team leader or chair a committee, be able to articulate sound middle-level philosophy in speech and in writing, understand and implement accepted child psychology and learning theory, and participate in Talent Night—at least.

The "I teach seventh grade science—to above average students only" stuff isn't going to do it. The teacher who still thinks that only the custodian should empty the classroom waste basket, and only the assistant principal deal with tough kids is not functioning at an optimal level. Every staff member is ultimately part of, and responsible for, the entire program. Administrators can exemplify that by carrying furniture, picking up trash, teaching a class, inviting *all* staff to in-service and staff meetings, getting rid of their own reserved parking spaces, repainting the teachers' lounge, dancing with the kids at the dance. We did all those things and more. When that message of group accountability is fully processed, "role-freeze" evaporates, kaizen evolves, and programs and people blossom.

It is also high time that all states adopted a middle-level certification enabling teachers to teach in more than one field without separate endorsements. Such certification should require extensive coursework in several liberal arts disciplines, however. The best way to integrate curriculum is through the teaching strengths of individual teachers performing as generalist teacher/learners conversant in several disciplines, expert in at least two.

Access to Modern Equipment

It is the 1990s. We hear much about teacher professionalism. How many teachers have their own real telephones? How many have unrestricted access to a phone within fifty feet? Until all teachers have something as basic as a telephone to use as they see fit, such talk of professionalization is absurd.

The same is true, in slightly less degree, of access to copiers and computers. Secretaries have access to all three of these things—and often teachers have to ask their permission to use any of them!

Stop Punching the Clock and Give up the Keys to the Kingdom

How many schools still monitor the comings and goings of their staff? How many administrators require teachers (and clerical people) to obtain permission to leave the building during the day—even on student-free time or for lunch? How many unions negotiate over time, as if their people were grocery clerks? How many staff have keys to their school so that they can work at night or on weekends?

In few professions are people required to punch the clock. In few professions are the comings and goings of staff monitored. Educators should be treated like adult professionals, just as they should behave like adult professionals. Bargaining so that one may leave school fifteen minutes after one's students, thus allowing no time for substantive afternoon meetings, or proactive planning, is not a professional practice. Professionals do not work seven-hour days.

As principal of a school I made certain that every staff person had keys to the front door. Having keys all over the place scares many administrators to death. They imagine all the things that can go wrong if the keys are lost, stolen, or misused. Principals think nothing of giving the master key to a newly-hired custodian in off the road, yet cannot imagine twenty-five-year veteran teachers with any keys but the ones to their class and the restroom.

In our situation there was not one single incident of theft or vandalism as a result of teachers having a key to *their* building. What's more, we routinely had teachers staying hours past required time, returning to the building to work at night, and coming in on weekends—all fantastic occurrences in typical schools.

Teachers all too quickly forget what it was like to be a student. Administrators forget what it was like to be a teacher. Issues of power and control are fought unnecessarily, tying up people and systems, slowing productivity, confusing communication.

Answer Every Phone Call

When you call a professional office or business, you do not get a busy signal, you do not get no answer, and you do not expect the office to be closed for the day at 3:45 P.M. None of these things happen in transformed schools either. Adequate phone systems, efficient answering, and office hours until 5:00 P.M. are the least we can do for our clients—the community we serve.

There is no inherent contradiction between an efficient organization and a humane environment. Quality is something too often lacking in our schools and in the larger culture. A humane business where quality is exemplified—from the front lawn to the letterhead on the stationery, from the spirited output of the kids to the friendly courtesy of the person answering the phone (within two rings)—is the kind of educational place we want for our children and for ourselves. The transformational middle-level school is such a place.

RECOGNITION OF STAFF

We spent some time talking about recognition as a component of student morale. It is essential for staff morale as well. Recognition also functions as an additional element of staff building, training, and retraining in the humane business. Getting teachers out to visit other programs, to conferences and workshops, and even to national conventions as often as possible is a proven way to stimulate and reward staff. Each year we took one veteran teacher to the ASCD Annual Conference with school travel funds. Such a fine conference has a great impact on teacher self-image and subsequent professionalization. When that teacher returns and reports to the group, it is an expansive experience for all.

Encouraging and enabling teachers to present at state and regional conferences is another powerful element in transformation. Such an experience is creative and regenerating for the teachers. Hosting such conferences and regular visitation days at your school is also a method of fostering staff growth through recognition and professional interactions.

"Hey, Okay!" Awards

Every staff member had two blank certificates at the beginning of the year to be given to anyone at any time for anything. We called them the "Hey, Okay!" Awards. Each staff meeting began with a presentation of "Hey, Okay!" Awards from anyone to anyone else. Making this a peer recognition program, not a principal recognition program, added a new element and made the awards unique, unpredictable, and fun.

Principal's Awards

It was also exciting and valuable to give awards each year to several staff members to complement the four student "Right Stuff" awards. Awards were given for Excellence in Teaching, Distinguished Service, and The Mary/Harry Sunshine Award for overall good cheer.

We had a notoriously tough, though earnest and hardworking, physical education teacher. She also served as athletic director and girls' middle school and high school track coach. When she received a Distinguished Service Award she told me through her tears that, "This is the first time in seventeen years anyone has honored me in this way."

We should never wait until people retire to let them know how much we value them. It is just as rich an experience for the veteran teacher or the long-time custodian, as it is for the wide-eyed seventh grader. It may be more so.

Professional Library

Set aside a space in the school where teachers and administrators can go to read articles and books, write in their journals, watch professional videotapes, listen to audiotapes, confer with colleagues. Have a case full of labelled, categorized copies of current articles on all aspects of transformational teaching/learning environments.

A teacher can pop in and pick up just what she/he is looking for on cooperative learning, or interdisciplinary units, or student morale. The principal can steer an interested parent or visitor to the professional library and hand them a strong article on the merits of teaming, or a description of the advisory program.

Maintaining a well-stocked professional library is a way of keeping focus on the task at hand, encouraging teachers to take productive breaks from their daily regimen, and providing teacher access to the best educational research and current thought. It tells the staff that what they are doing is valuable and assists them in kaizen.

A state-of-the-art professional library also includes videotapes and videotaping equipment. Teachers should have time and assistance in filming their classes and those of colleagues. It is such a powerful tool—far better than some observation checklist. This tremendous re-source is still not used to advantage in our schools. It was an area where we failed to do very much either, I might add. Perhaps this fits into the category of items that simply need to be mandatory, for the great value of self-taping is bound to be acknowledged once it occurs.

The Group Hug

We ended our full staff meeting with a group hug in the center of the large meeting room. Initially many staff resisted this. They did not embrace the idea of embracing one another. Once they actually got up and did it, smiles, laughs, and a tangible release of high energy resulted. Each time it was easier for the resisters to join the crowd. Some never really liked it, and one or two would slip away out the side door, however.

This was an area in which we took a calculated risk. We risked that our initial discomfort would give way to later growth of expression and greater feelings of commonality. With any but the most go-for-it staff, strong feelings of resistance will manifest. The process may backfire. I am still not certain if the gains for the larger group were worth the loss to those few who never felt free to participate. It raises the ongoing issues of when to move, who to include, working with highest or lowest common denominators, and so on. (We will deal with these issues in more depth in Chapters 11 and 12.)

I am convinced, however, that all those who stayed, those who even learned to look forward to this display of group affection, gained some-thing by touching each other in the way that we encourage them to touch the kids. This is another great way to break role-freeze, and to recognize one another's common humanity and need for affection, all at the same time.

"Just Win, Baby!"

Nordstrom says, "Use your best judgement at all times." The Oakland Raiders NFL football team says, "Just win, baby!" and it has been doing so consistently for twenty-five years. We might modify those slogans for a description of our actual teaching expectations to say something like: "All we expect is excellence; we do not care too much about exactly how we attain it."

The point is that if you are to treat teachers like professionals, establish a professional environment for them to work in, and recognize them as much as possible for their individual and collective strengths, it is wrong to break out the ponderous teacher handbook and turn to page 89, line up the observation checklists, and demand canned lessons from everyone.

In three years I never looked at a single lesson plan book. I had not forgotten how I often planned for my teaching/learning with five-minute scribble sessions on Friday afternoon. I was known to be well-organized and still am, but it does not manifest in that way. I am also spontaneous and do not need much direction, even from myself. Plan books never meant much to me. Some people swear by them. That is fine. Vive la différence. How a teacher prepares for teaching is that teacher's business alone. Principals spending hours checking lesson plans on Friday afternoons are wasting time and hamstringing their own staff.

The same approach is true for technique. We advocated cooperative learning in our school, but we never expected that every staff member would use it all the time (we did not want them too!), and we knew that some would never use it—and could still be terrifically effective. There are a lot of good things to do. Experienced teachers have thousands of techniques and gimmicks in their Trick Bag. Many of those techniques will come to the teacher intuitively in the moment. Many of them, if planned, will not work because Mars is no longer aligned with Venus and therefore Tuesday was "a no good horrible very bad day." The bottom line is the result, what is happening in the class, how the kids and teacher feel about this process, and what is being taught and really learned.

I did observe hundreds of classes and I did engage teachers in hundreds of discussions about what they were doing, why they were doing it, and how they might do it more effectively. We were stuck with an observation instrument we had not designed and we did use it, but we modified it, were flexible with it, and used many other means of evaluation and dialogue as well. The instrument was used as a map, not a blueprint. As a result, it did not paralyze us the way it might have.

We also encouraged (and finally mandated) teachers to observe at least four other classes each year and conference with the observed teacher. This was an increasingly helpful tool in opening communication, sharing information and ideas, breaking patterns of isolation, and moving to a synergistic, supportive organizational web.

All this observation in turn led to greater recognition than our teachers had ever known. It is flattering to a teacher to see other teachers encouraged by previous visitors to observe him/her. It is exciting to be in an open-door classroom setting where what you do each day is shared, and even celebrated, by your colleagues.

6

TEAMING

*"Win / win is based on the paradigm that there is
plenty for everybody, that one person's success
is not achieved at the expense or exclusion
of the success of others."*
—STEPHEN R. COVEY

We have been looking at elements of student and staff morale, professionalism, the "humane business" orientation, balance, wholeness,
and vision. Here we will consider how to establish patterns of interaction that support the pragmatic idealism outlined above. Before we
elaborate on this we have to add one essential ingredient—people. As
soon as we decide that we wish to enable people to work together, to
more fully share all aspects of the teaching/learning experience, we
need to move from the human isolation inherent in the old model. We
need something far more collaborative, something far more personally
and socially stimulating—and actually much more productive. We
must get ourselves into teams.

EVEN PRO TENNIS PLAYERS PLAY DAVIS CUP

When we think about it, virtually every human activity involves
some element of teamwork and cooperation at some point. With our
national mythology of rugged individualism this is hard for some of us
to accept. But even the most intrepid pioneer almost always worked in
collaboration with a family member, spouse, friend, or someone
needed along the route. Generally small determined bands were more
successful than lone individuals. Jamestown, Plymouth, New Amster-
dam, St. Augustine, and the opening of the West are among many clear
examples of this pattern of collaboration. (Still healthier exemplars of
human collaboration were the Native American tribes driven off and
eventually annihilated by the European colonizers.)

Then we turn to the entrepreneurs, the Carnegies and Rockefellers. When we study them in detail, they may not actually be particularly good role models, but even those fellows had to develop elaborate relationships, corporations finally, to accomplish what they intended.

Modern professional tennis players, Olympic athletes in solo sports, or concert pianists are examples of individuals functioning at a high success level without initial evidence of teamwork. Yet a closer look reveals that they too must rely on their peers, coaches, parents, friends, trainers, officials, agents, and so on in order to obtain and sustain significant success. The notion of a world of individuals (or nations!) competing with one another for the limited fruits of survival is another erroneous, obsolete, and even dangerous image. Genuinely successful people, judged both on financial *and* personal measures of well-being, are not usually cutthroat competitors, or social isolates. They are usually people-oriented with deep values, adaptability, and the skill to work cooperatively with a range of other individuals (Covey, 1990; Dyer, 1989; Kohn, 1991.)

THE UNCONSTRAINED WORLDVIEW

Like the idealists spoken of on the first page of this book, successful people generally subscribe to an "unconstrained" worldview. Such a view posits that there really is enough to go around, that the key to taking better care of people has more to do with improved attitudes, management, and distribution than it has to do with simple production.

Luis Machado, with his views on human intelligence potential, believes this, surely. Jerome Bruner, in his famous statement that virtually any person can learn virtually anything if taught appropriately, demonstrates such a belief. Mother Theresa not only believes this, but lives it, always somehow providing for everyone who comes her way. Of course her inspiration is the life of Jesus, the greatest proponent of such a view, who personally demonstrated that love is an infinite substance.

On a more material level, those developing alternatives to fossil fuels have an unconstrained worldview, having realized that the sun and wind have a long-term promise of plenty not supplied by oil. And what of the amazing miracle of the recently starving, penniless giant, India, now become an exporter of rice? Then there is the teacher in the classroom who knows in her/his bones that every single kid *could* be fully productive, every single kid *could* get an A in this course—and darn it, they just might!

THE NEED TO WIN

One salient reason for the variety of mental and physical illnesses rampant in our culture is the lack of genuine connection with others. We have long been acting on the questionable notion that human nature is essentially competitive. The schools reflect that thinking, with their student isolation, grading and ranking, competition, and win/lose systems. Our American culture is certainly competitive, often to absurd lengths, but is this a natural condition? Is self-seeking behavior any more "natural" than selfless behavior? Many people and many scholars would argue otherwise.

One noted proponent of fostering children's altruism in school settings is Alfie Kohn. His ample research of several hundred studies has convinced him that the assumption "that people are naturally and primarily selfish and will act otherwise only if they are coerced into doing so and carefully monitored," is severely limited. He does not deny our weaker side, but says that, "it is as natural to help as it is to hurt, that concern for the well-being of others often cannot be reduced to self-interest, that social structures predicated on human selfishness have no claim to inevitability—or even prudence."

I would imagine that anyone reading this book has at least as many prosocial feelings in a given day as antisocial ones, is far more prone to help someone in trouble than to take advantage, prefers harmony to discord, enjoys the company of others, gives to charity more often than steals, and has a definite, developed conscience. But so many of our systems maintain us in an independent state, promote competition, keep score even when we wish they did not.

The loss of a natural interdependence, the constant displacement through travel and job changes, the splitting up of the extended family, the lack of commitment to people, and the subsequent overreliance on things are elements of our uniquely American malaise. More stable, family-oriented, even tribal cultures, though replete with their own problems, have fewer of the ones we have: depression, anxiety, alienation, heart attacks, substance abuse, suicide, violence against one's own group, and the insane over-competitiveness that can make a simple pick-up basketball game, or a child's little league game a dangerous, ugly experience:

The Need to Win

When an archer is shooting for nothing
He has all his skill.
If he shoots for the brass buckle
He is already nervous.
If he shoots for a prize of gold
He goes blind
Or sees two targets —
He is out of his mind!

His skill has not changed. But the prize
Divides him. He cares.
He thinks more of winning
Than of shooting —
And the need to win
Drains him of power.

— CHUANG TZU

Over and over again corporate leaders are telling educators that one of their central concerns regarding their workers is *the ability to get along and work effectively with others* (Covey, Ball, 1991; Iacocca, 1991; Peters, 1987). The best reason to develop a quality experience based on teams and teamwork in our schools is not simply to satisfy the needs of American business, however, or even to destroy the so-called Japanese menace. The reason to do it is that it is simply a better process/product experience for all.

International business consultant Steven Covey has written a best-seller, *The 7 Habits of Highly Effective People.* In the book he speaks at length of the need for human psychoemotional maturation. He describes how successful people are able to move on a "Maturity Continuum" from dependence to independence to interdependence. "Interdependence is the paradigm of *we — we* can do it, *we* can cooperate, *we* can combine our talents and abilities and create something greater together."

TEAMING STRUCTURES

There are many ways of setting up teams. There are many variables of staff abilities and interests, certifications, student population, staff personalities, etc. that need to be considered. It is also important to consider practices in the other district schools in order to make sixth grade a natural transition between fifth and seventh (therefore like both fifth and seventh), and to make eighth grade a natural transition between seventh and ninth grade (therefore like both seventh and ninth). Assuming a sixth to eighth grade middle-level program, and some relatively sound elementary and high school practices on either end, we would recommend something along the following lines.

Student Numbers

Twenty students per section is optimal. Twenty-five students per section is okay. Numbers much beyond that should be resisted. Obviously current fiscal and spatial constraints will largely determine class size in all but the most sensible and/or wealthy districts. Classes can function up to thirty and even beyond, if mere functioning is all you desire (or if there is additional teaching assistance and giant classrooms). Strong team structures require ratios of approximately 20–25:1, if at all possible. The splitting of these sections in order to create reasonable advisory group sizes will also necessitate keeping the ratios manageable.

Staff Numbers and Subject Assignments

We prefer two-person sub-teams at sixth grade (forty to fifty students), rolled into a larger four-person team (eighty to one hundred students). Each sub-team has elementary-certified teachers able to teach at least two subjects. Generally a social studies/language arts person and a math/science person is a simple way to divide responsibility. However, they may divvy it up differently, through team-teaching the whole student group social studies, both teaching a math section, and splitting up science and language arts, for example. Any way that enables teachers to spend adequate time in those four "Core" disciplines is fine. Allowing more or less time for more or less important subjects or units will also depend on interdisciplinary approaches, use of the block Core time, etc.

This format provides a closeness for, and to, the younger students, allowing them to deal with only two adults in their Core classes. This is an arrangement that is hopefully more similar to the elementary one they have just come from. (Note our earlier concern about secondary-ation of elementary programs.) Being part of the larger four-member team enables the teachers to coordinate planning and curriculum, use of facilities, trips, field experiences, guest speakers, films, etc. It provides additional social options for teachers and students as well.

In seventh grade a two-, three-, or four-person team is fine, depending again on variables of students, spaces, and teacher certifications—which usually become more critical, as this grade level is often considered "secondary" and therefore specialized in many states. Obviously two- or four-person teams are easier logistically, but three will work, just not as neatly—and every teacher may not have every student in the team and vice versa.

Eighth grade is a transition from seventh to ninth, and therefore it is the grade most likely to have one teacher per Core subject, reflecting more of the high school scenario to come. Again, creative flexibility should be employed in all staffing/teaming structuring at all grade levels.

Vertical Student-Teacher Teams

Developing vertical teams is something not done as often, though it has great merit. In such an arrangement, a team of teachers would work with the same team of students for more than one year, sixth and seventh, seventh and eighth, or even sixth to eighth. That way the students could even remain in the same "house" or area of the building for more than one year. The marvelous middle-level program on Long Island at Shoreham Wading River Middle Schol uses a modification of such an arrangement. In SWR students remain in the same pod with the same advisor for three years. They have a new two-person team for the four core subjects in sixth, seventh, and eighth grades. These six teachers function in a vertical team, and pair in a horizontal, grade-level team as well. Such a format requires strong teachers with diverse abilities and a go-for-it attitude.

One argument often heard for not keeping students with teachers for more than one year is that it would prove untenable regarding students who had conflicts with certain teachers. This is a thin argument on several grounds. First, you could always transfer the student to another team, as can be done in mid-year or at virtually any time when there are apparently unresolvable personality conflicts. Second, it allows the *negative* thinking that students and teachers cannot get along well for more than one year, or improve difficult relationships, to supersede the *positive* thinking that many teachers and students actually get along quite well, and would only do better with more time to work together. Third, it assumes that there will be more than a few student-teacher conflicts in the course of a year. In strong, supportive teaming situations this is rarely the case.

My own experience of teaching the same students for up to three consecutive years confirms in my mind that it can be an excellent experience for all. The time saved simply from not needing to get to know one another in the beginning of the second year is invaluable in and of itself. The depth of the resulting relationships is another wonderful element.

Inclusionary Nature of Student Teams

Each team should have a *full range of student abilities* within it. It is antithetical to the team concept to have teams perceived as "better" or "worse." Putting all the G/T students, or all the remedial students, on one team would establish such a perception.

In our program we had all the LD students on one team. The team had a full range of students, however, with the LD kids constituting 25–30% of the team and mixed into several classes. The LD resource teacher(s) was(were) also on that team. That teacher both pulled kids out for individual and small group attention and worked alongside them in their regular classes, depending on factors determined by the teaching team. Such a format enabled us to mainstream the kids (and teacher) quite well, house them in the team area, maintain constant communication and support with the LD teacher, and de-stigmatize their program. No Leper Colonies. In addition, again to provide real and perceived balance, we had all the SD (or school-disabled, non-labelled) kids on the other team in each grade. They also received resource help, but through our Learning Lab. (A full discussion of that program appears in Chapter 10.)

Team Spirit

In well-functioning teams, a team ethic and team spirit is fostered by the teachers. Teams have their own names, identities, slogans, rituals, recognitions, and team zones or houses. The more teachers play into this team theme stuff, the more fun they have with it, the more kids will buy into it and make it go.

Teams can have their own weekly or monthly awards, celebrations, trips, service projects, mascots, clean-up zones, etc. Many successful middle-level teams establish partnerships with local businesses and obtain tee-shirts, materials, and even expensive equipment in exchange for service, public relations benefits, and advertising for the business.

Team spirit and student morale will be naturally abetted because housing students together by team breaks the often large, imposing, symmetrical, and impersonal middle-level building into smaller, more user-friendly parts. Many middle-level schools do orientations for fifth graders prior to their sixth grade year. At these orientations, students visit their team houses, as well as the entire school, and they visit with their team teachers for the first time.

The kids can also try the lockers out, as a new middle schooler's worst nightmare is LMF: Locker Manipulation Failure. A neat student morale trick is to start each year with several padlocks and keys on hand. Giving them to the few students who just cannot get it (LD or EMR kids will sometimes have especially difficult times with this) will save staff daily bother. Orientations, back-to-school nights, and special team activities that include parents and relatives are all excellent ways to build team spirit.

Teacher Team Accountability

If a team of teachers is to be a genuine team, there must be group accountability. In the daily team meeting time the group plans all the workings of the team, develops a team approach to student morale issues, coordinates interdisciplinary units and themes, manipulates the scheduled blocks of Core time, arranges for team activities, even establishes team evaluation procedures and shares the reporting process on each student.

Virtually all the tasks previously done by the single teacher in isolation are now done in concert with the other members. The tasks still done individually might be those pertaining to individual class planning and research in a particular field, classroom maintenance and decor, parental contacts not involving the other team members, coordination of special projects or activities involving one or two teachers, and so on.

A practice we developed that greatly enhanced the concept of team accountability and interdependence was the *Team Observation Process*. We created a format for a Team Observation in which the principal schedules a week-long visitation with one team several weeks in advance. The principal and the Team Leader then meet at the beginning of the visit and also at the end of the week. The team recommends several areas of focus for the principal, and the principal might also note one or two areas. Observation and feedback on those areas serve as the basis for the visitation process. (Of course an assistant principal may participate as the administrator in place of, or in addition to, the principal.)

Each day during that week the administrator observes several different classes and joins the team members for their daily meeting. During the week the administrator and each team member also hold individual conferences to focus on teaching/learning practices to be viewed. The administrator might participate in some manner during the week, teach a class, read to students, join an activity, sit in on a parent conference, or the like. After the visitation period, a lengthy written report by the administrator speaks to the areas observed, as well as general impressions of the team process, the performance of students, and the specific contributions of team members. After the report is distributed to team members, the administrator joins them in a final team meeting to discuss the report and its implications. The report is positive in tone and objective in language, offering special advice in areas of requested focus if that is necessary.

This becomes a rich and rewarding process. Teachers much prefer it to the old individual, isolated conferences that often come months apart from one another and do not relate to the team process or the increasingly interdisciplinary nature of the curriculum. Elements of it that I would emphasize are:

- the administrator's commitment of time to the team
- the primary identification of areas of focus by the team, not the administrator
- the writing of a lengthy, involved narrative to use as a basis for feedback, reference, and further discussion

Teacher Team Leadership

The issue of who, if anyone, is to lead the team, is a complex one. Like many complex issues there is no single answer. It is best to develop a practice that is most comfortable for your organization—and to continually evaluate and improve it.

We felt that having designated Team Leaders (TLs) in the initial stages of our program was appropriate. What's more we solicited faculty desire both as to who wanted to be a TL and whom teachers thought would make a good TL. We were able to use virtually every strongly recommended and volunteer teacher—and this usually became the same talent pool, for those who were most interested were generally seen as leaders by their peers already. The TLs had one-year terms, and the opportunity to volunteer again at the end of the year. I reserved the final right to both appoint TLs and assign teachers to teams. I did this with much feedback from teachers, much sharing, and much thought. As a result our process, after the somewhat awkward beginnings, evolved very nicely. By the third year virtually every teacher wanted to stay in the team he/she was in, supported his/her team leaders, and gave the team high marks in process/product.

TLs have responsibility for team leadership and record keeping (which they are free to delegate), they serve as primary spokespersons in parent-team conferences when that is appropriate, they function as the contact persons for their teams, and they serve on the Teaching Learning Committee (TLC), which is comprised of all TLs and the principal. This committee is the primary policy-making group for the school. It meets once every two weeks for approximately ninety minutes after school.

Compensation for a TL consisted of a modest cash stipend of a few hundred dollars, one additional planning period, and a fair share of status and increased responsibility and visibility in the school. The goal is for everyone to eventually develop the confidence and the capability to serve as a TL. On a professional and highly productive staff this is fully possible within a matter of years (see Appendix). Some schools and organizations simply rotate team leadership annually or bi-annually as a matter of course. What is more important than the format is that there is a solid, established, productive team process and many opportunities for individual leadership abilities to emerge and flourish.

Teacher Team Efficacy

It takes a while for any team to gel. Good teams become such through time and effort and mistakes. Putting people together is only the beginning of team creation. After that they will need feedback, information, supplies and equipment, assistance, advice, occasional mediation, and above all—time.

Setting up a team office in a central location, with file cabinets, teacher desks, telephone, and coffee really helps promote the team ethic. We provided all our teachers with portable teaching stations in their classrooms, then moved the individual desks to the team offices. This way teachers gravitated naturally to the team office; it left classrooms available for other classes if needed, yet the teacher usually still had a private classroom space to return to if/when that was desired.

It may be interesting to note here that the classic faculty room bitch session may actually be a distortion of a natural social need. Teachers find themselves placed together at random in the faculty room due to the vagaries of the schedule, but they may have almost nothing in common to talk about professionally—teaching different courses and sections of courses to different kids in different places. Yet they do have the human need to converse—and it can become quite negative when there is no common focus. Often such conversation turns against the "bad" kids in the school. This is especially evident in an ineffectual school where student and teacher morale is down and the two groups are in an adversarial relationship.

When the school is transformed, and when teachers and students are in teams, all suddenly have tremendous commonality. Then when teachers get together to eat and talk (more and more in the team room, rather than the distant faculty lounge), the conversation naturally revolves around their common experience, with each other and with the kids—and quite often it becomes remarkably positive.

Time for Success

By scheduling daily individual planning time *and* daily team planning time for virtually all teachers, we were able to provide the most essential (and generally most elusive) element of school transformation—*time*. In the next chapter you will see that all of our teachers had two and a half hours a day free from students, when team planning, individual planning, and lunch were tallied. Our sixth grade teachers had the final two and a half hours of the school day free of students— every day. This was done with no additional staff.

What's more, teachers had no more than five classes, and quite a few had four, plus a duty. Teachers with five classes had no duty, except for some of the sixth grade teachers who rotated on lunch duty throughout the year. No one ever had hall duty. With a physically active administration, and high student morale, that is not necessary. It frees teachers to do the two main things they should be doing—facilitating teaching/ learning and planning for it.

Teams should stay together indefinitely if they are functioning well, or at least progressing. If there is adequate care given to balancing teams initially, they should be able to become successful eventually, no matter where they are at first. However, they certainly can be modified, even disassembled, if they remain ineffectual over a full one or two years, and new staffing arrangements are available and/or necessary due to hiring and attrition.

Deciding on a team's efficacy and fate can be a tough call for the principal, as teachers will get comfortable with one another and not necessarily want to move, even if the team is not exactly humming. Dialogue with team leaders and members, much observation, and clear thought are all required for optimum team grouping and regrouping. If a team is not doing particularly well, its members need specific support, feedback, and even experiences in group process, similar to that given to students in cooperative learning models. In fact, training teachers in cooperative learning for their students is a fine way to develop group process skills at the teacher team level (Brandt, 1987).

Teaming is perhaps *the* critical element of a transformational middle-level program. It would be wonderful if the concept spread more widely to high schools and elementary schools as well. It is a powerful force when thoughtfully developed and properly utilized. In order for it to be optimally effective the structure should include:

- a strong interdisciplinary component
- daily team teacher planning time
- staff involvement in team staffing procedures
- a designated leader or contact person
- team representation on the major committee(s)
- full range of student ability levels on each team
- defined team zones, areas, or "houses" in building

- manageable student numbers
- flexible staffing, and remixing of team members if needed
- much discussion, time, and training prior to implementation
- team accountability and a Team Observation Process

In addition to these key factors, we have noted that the schedule must reflect and support the team process, not deny or constrain it. Teaming and schedule are tightly and effectively interwoven in a working middle-level program. Schedule, the most technically complex of all these issues, will be explored in the next chapter.

7
SCHEDULE

"To effect the quality of the day,
that is the highest of the arts."
— HENRY DAVID THOREAU

OUR GOD, OUR SCHEDULE

In the typical school the schedule has a life of its own. It is a mysterious, dark force. In the beginning staff members, fully grown adults, pay homage to this unknowable power. It offers a semblance of purpose in the turbulent secondary school regimen. They hope that perhaps it can shape their lives into meaning, perhaps somehow set them free to teach. Over time their expectant worship gives way to doubt. They begin to believe that the schedule is The Schedule and that there is nothing mortal teachers can do to change it. Even the bravest, most stalwart principal moves sheepishly among her people, powerless to combat The September Monster.

This is unfortunate. The typical secondary schedule is extremely problematic. It greatly constrains the entire organization, prohibiting all manner of G/I. How does it do that? Why is it allowed to? Don't some schools do it differently? Is there no alternative to this rigid, merciless being that assumes a life of its own in a school? Let us take a look first at the downside. Many educators and parents do not even recognize what the schedule does, and how limiting an inflexible, obsolete one can be.

WHY THE SCHEDULE IS BAD

Can you imagine an adult working environment in which each worker changes activities, work stations and supervisors every forty-

five minutes, eight to ten times per day, all day long? Each worker has
no work station of his own, but rather carries tools on the back in a
sack, or stashes them in a metal locker, returning to it all day long,
from various parts of the work environment. What is more, each of the
eight to ten separate activities has little or nothing to do with any of the
others. Each worker travels and works in isolation, meeting friends
along the way, but following an individual routine unconnected to
anyone else. Social needs are met through snatched conversations in
the corridors and in the hyper-rush, feeding frenzy at lunch. Bells
sound periodically and continually to keep the workers alert and moving properly. The worker has virtually no choice in what to work on in
any given work day.

From the supervisor's view it is not appreciably better, and it might
be worse. Each may deal with as many as 150 workers or more in the
day, have six, seven, or more assignments, change activities as often as
the workers, work in equal isolation, have even fewer opportunities to
interact with peers socially or professionally, and have little or no ongoing sharing or evaluation of his/her work process.

If you read educational literature this may sound all too familiar
(George, 1983; Goodlad, Jacobs, 1989; Silberman, 1970). The secondary school model has been decried for some time. Decades. Yet it persists. The middle school movement arose in large measure as an antidote to the junior high school, an essentially secondary school model
(George). But how many "middle schools," despite other innovations
and attempted G/I processes, are still plagued with this rigid, linear,
sequential eight to ten period schedule and its accompanying organizational structure?

Within such a system students and teachers become dulled to all
kinds of possibilities, while developing many questionable behaviors:

- They become increasingly goal-, future-, and product-oriented.
- They forget about the connections between different subject
  areas or experiences.
- Courses are not taught or learned, they are "covered."
- Speed is in, quality is out.
- Many things are interrupted, many never completed.
- Control of the process is abdicated to the clock and bell.
- Personal relationships are continually compromised and
  sacrificed in the name of "efficiency."

- It is difficult to develop or maintain student-teacher connections.
- Deep, persistent feelings of confusion, meaninglessness, and isolation set in for many people.
- Time becomes the great enemy of all.

For years we have known of a variety of school scheduling formats. Several of them offer effective alternatives to the traditional, symmetrical eight to ten period (including lunch, homeroom, and activity periods) schedule. Modular, block, rotational, and variable schedules have all been implemented in schools. Many have met with success. Yet the traditional one persists, despite its severe limitations. There are a few reasons that it does, including these:

(1) It is simple, and easily understood.
(2) It is typical, and easily translated.
(3) It is "the way things have been done."
(4) Most school personnel know remarkably little about the scheduling systems in place, and even less about modifying them. This is even more true of school boards.

Are these sound reasons, however, or are they excuses?

THE SCHEDULE SHOULD SUPPORT THE PROGRAM, NOT CONSTRAIN IT

Given acceptance of the problematical nature of The Schedule, given acceptance of our need to make schools more functional *and* more humane, given acceptance of a true team structure for students and staff, we have to turn the process around somehow. When devising a schedule, we have to first determine what it is we wish to happen in the organization, what kinds of productivity and outcomes on all levels of human endeavor we wish to encourage and sustain. Then we must create a system that is harmonious, one that is congruent with our goals.

What we have decided at this point is that we want a school program that is

- balanced and whole
- collaborative and professional

- flexible and functional
- high quality and humane
- person-centered

Our schedule must not only help us get there — it must guarantee that we can get there, and that we will stay there.

In order for such a schedule to be developed and sustained, again *attitude* is the key ingredient. Transforming a schedule will be technically complex and politically sensitive. Many special interest groups will cling to what they have, even if it is not particularly good, rather than take a chance on something new.

Many school programs have schedules designed around PE times, or when the reading teacher can come from another building, or what the science department chairperson wants, or what the hassled assistant principal in charge of schedule is able to come up with on his wall chart each spring, or what some scheduling consultant who knows little of school transformation is punching up out of a second-rate computer program designed by someone else who knows little of school transformation. (All too often we misuse our sophisticated modern technology so that it only enables us *to do the wrong thing better*.)

The schedule will be transformed as the program is transformed, through the continual efforts and best thinking of a host of tuned-in professionals with a "Just do it!" attitude. It will also go through many phases, revisions, trials and errors, glitches, and snafus. But when staff members evolve to the point where they understand their place in the schedule, and the philosophy driving the schedule, then amazing synergy develops, and the schedule becomes organic — fluid and alive.

TAKE THE TOP OFF YOUR HEAD

As an example of how a staff can grow in this manner, one year we had gone four months on our bell-less schedule depicted in Figures 5, 6, and 7. (Additional schedule formats and a 5–8 schedule are provided in the Appendix.) The bus arrival times had been all over the place all year, and many buses were still delivering kids too early, and arriving early to pick them up as well. We realized that it would be easier if we could shift the schedule back about eight minutes. We sent out a notice one week in advance that we would do this, and we enclosed the new

Grade 6

Period	1	2	3	4	L /5	6	7
X	HR	C	O	R	E (ADV)	Lunch/Social	Explorat.	PE
Y	HR	C	O	R	E (ADV)	Lunch/Social	PE	Ex/Bnd

Grade 7

Period	1	2	3	4	L/ 5	6	7
X	C O R E	PE	ELECT (ADV)	Social/ Lunch	C O R E
Y	C O R E	Band/El	PE (ADV)	Social/ Lunch	C O R E

Grade 8

Period	1	2	3	4	L/5	6	7	8
X	EL	PE	C O R E (ADV)	Lun	C O R E	EL
Y	PE	Band/EL	C O R E (ADV)	Lun	C O R E	EL

Code: X,Y = Teams   CORE = Math, Science, Social Studies, Lang. Arts
EL = Electives   ADV = Advisory (Once a week)   HR = Homeroom
Note: Periods 48-55 minutes in length. 8th grade: 5 minute longer day, shorter HR time, no social time at lunch, 2 elective per. instead.

FIGURE 5. Middle-Level Schedule: Students (Block, Period, and Rotational).

Grade 6

Period	1	2	3	4	L /5	6	7
X	HR	C O R E (ADV)				Lunch/ Duty	Team Plan	Indiv.
Y	HR	C O R E (ADV)				Lunch/ Duty	Team Plan	Indiv.

Grade 7

Period	1	2	3	4	L/ 5	6	7
X	C O R E	Team Plan	EL/IP (ADV)	Lunch	C O R E
Y	C O R E	EL/IP	Team Plan	Lunch	C O R E

Grade 8

Period	1	2	3	4	L/5	6	7	8
X	EL	Team	C O R E (ADV)		Lun	C O R E		I P
Y	Team	Band/EL	C O R E (ADV)		Lun	C O R E		I P

Code: X,Y = Teams   CORE = Math, Science, Social Studies, Lang. Arts
EL = Electives   ADV = Advisory (Once a week)   HR = Homeroom
IP = Individ. Plan   Team = Team Plan

Note: In 7th grade a few Core teachers may teach electives 3rd or 4th and have IP after school. All teachers stay 45+ min. approx.

FIGURE 6. Middle-Level Schedule: Teachers (Block, Period, and Rotational).

Grade 6

```
Advisory . . . . . . . . . . . 7:50– 8:00
Core . . . . . . . . . . . . . . 8:05–11:55
Lunch . . . . . . . . . . . . .12:00–12:20
Social . . . . . . . . . . . . .12:20–12:28
EX/PE . . . . . . . . . . .12:30– 1.25
PE/EX . . . . . . . . . . . 1:30– 2:25
```

Grade 7

```
Advisory . . . . . . . . . . . 7:50– 8:00
Core 1 . . . . . . . . . . . . 8:05–10:00
PE/ELECT . . . . . . . . .10:05–11:00
ELECT/PE . . . . . . . . .11:05–12:00
Social . . . . . . . . . . . . .12:05–12:18
Lunch . . . . . . . . . . . . .12:18–12:40
Core 2 . . . . . . . . . . . .12:45– 2:28
```

Grade 8

```
Advisory . . . . . . . . . . . 7.50– 7:55
PE/ELECT . . . . . . . . . 8:00– 8:50
ELECT/PE . . . . . . . . . 8:55– 9:45
Core 1 . . . . . . . . . . . . 9:50–11:30
Lunch . . . . . . . . . . . . .11:35–11:55
Core 2 . . . . . . . . . . . .12:00– 1:40
ELECTIVE . . . . . . . . . 1:45– 2:33
```

SCHEDULE NOTES

-- One team has PE when other has EXP or ELECTIVE.
3 Bands meet every day: 6th -- 12:30-1:25, 7th --
11:05-12:00, 8th -- 8:55-9:45

-- After school Enrichment in Arts, Computer, Tech.
for interested students 2 days per week. (This
provides additional experience for Band students.)

-- 6-9 Week Exploratories (6th): Art, Music, Tech.,
Home Ec, Computer, Drama

-- Semester Electives (7th): Art, Chorus, Tech.,
Home Ec, Computer, Drama, Other

-- Semester Electives (8th): Art, Chorus, Tech.,
Home Ec, Computer, Drama, Journalism, Jazz Band,
Handbells, Literary Mag, Yearbook, Other

-- Full Year Electives (8th): French, Spanish, Latin,
Band (6, 7, 8)

* *Teachers control schedule--modify, flip/flop,
rearrange as they see fit.*

FIGURE 7. *Time Frames for Middle-Level Schedule (Figures 5 and 6).*

69

schedule minutes. We sent out a reminder the day before. Then on D-Day we shifted the entire bell-less schedule by eight minutes, lunch times by five minutes, and we threw in a few other needed minor adjustments while we were at it. There was no problem. Just none. No complaints either. The next day we went sailing right along. The staff had made one of those paradigm shifts. We were no longer paralyzed by the schedule, by all the things that we could not do. We had taken the top off our heads.

THE SCHEDULE TRANSFORMED

Our transformed schedule will look and act very differently from that nasty old monster. It will be flexible, provide varied blocks of time, establish academic Core periods, be organic and developmental, allow for teacher control and adaptability, prove stimulating for students, make the day slower and gentler, promote meaningful relationships between students and staff, encourage deeper involvement with few interruptions, and provide direction *and* variety of choice for students without creating a hodgepodge of unrelated, shallow teaching/learning experiences.

Schedules That Serve a Program

We have created clock-watching, agitated, reactive, short-term thinking students and teachers in our schools. One may stand at the front door of a school at 3:15 and watch the teaching staff come out en masse, like auto workers finishing a shift. "Contract says we're done. Let's go home." To a person they complain that they do not have enough time for planning and development of new approaches. They leave every day twenty minutes after their students.

When our bell-less schedule was up and running in the new building we moved into, we had a closet full of clocks we had ordered for classrooms, but not yet installed. When we began installing them, teachers in the first couple of rooms asked us why—because they no longer felt the need for clocks. So we sent out a note telling teachers that we had clocks and would put them up for whoever wanted one. Guess what? No takers. We got a refund on about sixty new wall clocks. We spent it on plants instead. (Now, one of our teachers has read this and insists it happened that way because the clocks were so ugly, nobody would dare display one. Hmmm. . . .)

The transformational schedule will provide students with:

- blocks of Core academic time
- staggered release times for all grades
- homeroom/advisory daily, one advisory period weekly
- rotations on advisory period so that it does not hit the same class each week
- daily PE/health time
- daily elective/exploratory time
- a full band period during the school day each day for all three grades[1]
- two electives daily for eighth graders
- three different lunch periods — no lines
- a total students-in-cafeteria time of sixty minutes
- twenty-minute social time for sixth and seventh graders
- bus release on a stagger — sixth graders first
- an extra elective period for eighth grade

This last is obtained by eliminating post-lunch social time (save twenty minutes), which students realize is not necessary when they have an additional elective period, shortening homeroom/advisory period from ten to five minutes (save five minutes), and rotation of electives on a fourteen out of fifteen day sequence, with Core time expanding each way — east to "eat" first period one week and second period the second week, and west to "eat" eighth period the third week (please see Figure 5). The resultant time period gained provides for advisory on Wednesdays.

The transformational schedule will provide teachers with:

- blocks of Core academic time
- staggered release times for all grades
- advisory groups of twelve to fifteen students per staff member
- rotations on advisory period so that it does not hit the same class each week
- daily team planning time
- daily individual planning time

---

[1]Another solution is to have performing groups take earlier and/or later bus runs with high school and/or elementary students. Holding performing groups in an early or late period eliminates all conflicts with other exploratory, elective, or activity involvements and also provides flex time on both ends of the day for a host of other activities, extra help, etc.

- additional planning period for Team Leaders
- five assigned periods per day
- only four classes and a duty for several
- no duty periods for most
- four periods of academic Core classes for Core teachers

In order to obtain the four academic classes, and not hire additional people to teach electives and exploratories in support of the teachers we already have in those areas, we sacrifice on class size somewhat. But in taking a first glance at this schedule one might assume that it requires *more* staff than a secondary-type plug-'em-in-the-holes schedule. This is not the case.

When we went to this scheduling plan we actually had a *higher* total student:faculty ratio than in previous years. (Establishing ratio by simply dividing total students by total teaching staff we went from 10.8:1 to 12.6:1.) Our class sizes in Core courses went from a range of approximately eighteen to twenty-five to a range of approximately twenty-two to twenty-eight. As it was a matter of trading larger classes for one less class in many instances, this arrangement was quite acceptable to most of our teachers and had no negative impact on student achievement (please see Figures 6 and 7).

I believe that generally twenty-five is the key number for reference regarding class size at the middle level. It is when classes get over twenty-five that certain pressures become more pronounced, that one feels the bodies, that the energy can become more frenetic simply due to spatial limitations. It is important to remember, though, that when there is a more people-centered approach in a school, when there is strong support for presently less-capable students through special services and a positive evaluation system (please see Chapters 9 and 10 Grading and Grouping), when student morale is high, and when there is an active *advisory* program, class size in and of itself is less important. Ideally we would have maintained the original ratio and kept all Core classes to a maximum of twenty-five. Smaller class size is something worth struggling for.

ADVISORY: BUILDING STUDENT-STAFF FRIENDSHIPS

We have alluded to *advisory* several times thus far. This is such an integral component of the transformational school that we need to describe it in detail. It is included in the Schedule chapter because consistent and ample time for it must be provided. Just as teacher teams cannot function without regular team planning time and emphasis, so too with advisory.

Advisory groups are heterogeneous. They are manageable in size, as small as staffing permits. By using virtually every professional staff member, including media specialists, physical education teachers, certified assistant teachers, special education teachers, art teachers, etc., a ratio of twelve to fifteen students per staff member can be attained. This also pulls into the central school experience many staff who otherwise would not be as hooked into kids and programs.

Some schools ask their administrators and counselors to take advisories. In our schedule we feel it to be impractical to have those key individuals tied up during the first part of every school day. We feel that we are not able to provide consistent experience for our advisory kids, that they would have advisors in and out of homeroom too often. In an extremely staid or small school this would surely prove beneficial, however.

Assigning Students to Advisors

We assign kids to staff based on two major factors. The first is physical proximity of the staff members' advisory space to the house of the students in that advisory. This is more important for sixth graders than it is for eighth graders and is factored in accordingly when spaces are assigned. This is one way of breaking the larger building into smaller pieces for students. It is inadvisable to send sixth graders all over the building for homeroom each morning. Space is at a premium when every student is accounted for in a 12–15:1 setting, so advisories often do meet in neutral zones, dividing larger spaces like a media center, cafetorium, gym, etc. If such a space is needed for some sixth grade advisories, take the one closest to the sixth grade house.

The second major factor is whether the student will also see the staff person during the school day, or year. This is one good way of building relationships. We make sure that half of the teacher's first Core class is that teacher's advisory group. Then it is a matter of finding the most appropriate non-Core staff person to take the other half of the group. Again, sixth graders would have preference here, as they know no one coming in. Eighth graders have already dealt with virtually every staff person by that time, so they are easiest to place.

Some schools assign advisors and they remain with their advisory for the three years. This has clear benefits in terms of depth of relationship. Logistically it is far more cumbersome, however, with either teachers or students travelling back into other grades' houses for advisory. This works best in a program when the teachers move with the students each year and would be an added benefit to such programs.

Thinking flexibly, remember that once a student is assigned to advisory, it is no more fixed in stone than any class assignment. If over time it appears that a student might be more successful in a different advisory, make the switch. Personality conflicts will happen, people will clash. Often a simple switch to a teacher more inclined to that student will instantly redeem a difficult situation. If a student complains that all her friends are in a different group, listen to that student. Exceptions are best resolved when they are dealt with as exceptions, not stifled or ignored because of our fear of a stampede that usually does not materialize.

"I'm a Teacher, Not a Counselor: What Do I Do?"

There is a lot of uncertainty when the concept of advisory is first introduced to staff. Not only are teachers afraid that they will be asked to psychoanalyze kids, but counselors are even more fearful that their role will be usurped or even replaced. It is wise to include counselors in the R&D stages to enable them to understand the program. Once they do, they will see the benefits to the school and to themselves. Why?

Advisory is an opportunity for staff to develop a "significant other" status with a select group of students. When this occurs, the students begin to take a host of relatively minor things to that staff member, and this frees guidance counselors to do what they do best, and that is deal with the far more complex psychoemotional issues plaguing students in stress.

The advisor functions like a good homeroom teacher, but has half the students to deal with, and very specific responsibilities. The advisor handles lost lunch tickets, forgotten homework, what upsetting thing was said on the bus, jammed lockers, who won the game, when the chess club meets again, what we are doing next Friday during the Team festival. This is what the traditional homeroom teacher did.

But the advisor becomes more attuned to the students and comes to see them in a special way. One responsibility our advisors assumed was to place a welcoming telephone call to each of their advisees and advisees' parents prior to the opening of school each year. Another was to personally monitor the completion of our complex report card, to distribute it, and to go over the contents with advisees prior to its going home. A third task was to contact each advisee's home once per marking period, regardless of advisee academic status.

The advisor also troubleshoots. Once the kids are known, the advisor looks for signs of discontent, anticipates problems, monitors progress, reminds Joey that the Budweiser shirt is inappropriate for school, comforts Sara on the death of her dog, notices that Lisa's eyes are kind of red and she is acting too giddy, maybe makes a phone call home to check mother's perception of things.

This is where the counselor and, possibly, administrator come in, with the support of the advisor and with information the advisor provides. The counselor is going to deal with the deeper, more dangerous issues of possible substance abuse, trauma over divorce, persistent attendance problems, and anger that is spilling over into violent acts. Rather than replace the counselor or the assistant principal, the advisor becomes a terrific help in identifying major difficulties. Then, working in concert, the advisor can become a large part of the agreed upon plan of action.

These examples have to do with the relationship between the advisor and advisee. The larger group process is an equally important part of the equation. Handling this aspect well is essential in an effective advisory program.

"This Is School, Not Group Therapy: What Do We Do?"

Once a week the whole group comes together for a time of at least one class period. What happens during this time is based upon several factors. Among them are the experience and desire of the staff member, the attitudes and interests of the different students, the advisory curriculum, the time of the year, what is happening in the larger Team, current events in the world outside, and so on.

The purpose of the longer advisory period is to develop group skills, to learn more about one another, to feel the support of the group, to learn more about ourselves, and best of all to do something meaningful for people outside the advisory group. Advisories evolve over the course of a year. Advisors evolve as they do advisory over time, and kids become more adept at group process and group accountability as they function in advisories through several grades.

Sending a Message of Service

One problem we solved through advisory was developing an effective Student Government Association (SGA). We always had trouble finding time for them to meet, as they were so busy after school, and lunch time meetings were short and often unproductive as the students resented loss of their social time. The SGA students did not have quite enough to do for us to make SGA an elective class, however. Those kids would not have wanted to give up something else to do it anyway. So we put them all in the same advisory. Because we wanted heterogeneity, we added other kids too. That just did not work well, however. Whenever there was an SGA involvement, and there often was, the advisory was divided. No good.

Rather than fight it, we made one advisory SGA only, and the kids and their advisor really ran with it. As we all came to see their role primarily as one of service, it was fine that they all worked together in this mode. There was no apparent resentment on the part of other students or elitist attitudes on the part of the SGA kids. Finally having the time to learn to function as a service group was just what they needed to become an effective student leadership team for the first time. They set a fine example of service for the other students too.

Evolution of Advisory

When many or all of the advisories in the school have taken on service projects as a central part of their advisory experience, then it is clear the advisory has evolved to a high level schoolwide. When many of those service projects are being done in the community outside of the school—clean-up campaigns, adopt-a-grandparent, adopt-an-elementary school class, building a playground, serving meals-on-wheels, assisting with a voter registration drive, etc.—they should be celebrated and publicized. This becomes uplifting for the students and staff and a fabulous public relations vehicle for the school program as well. Speaking of vehicles, purchasing (or leasing) a van large enough to carry an advisory group is a great investment. It could carry the basketball team too and soon pay for itself.

It will be helpful when beginning an advisory program to spend a lot of time focusing on why, what, and how prior to implementation. It will also prove worthwhile to develop a philosophical statement and a curriculum document that serve as guidelines for staff in getting started. The curriculum for advisory should be general and flexible, allowing for less experienced, or less creative, teachers to rely on it, without its impeding more experienced, more creative teachers.

Transforming a schedule is not as hard as one might think, and I hope the mapping done in this chapter demonstrates that. It is not easy, though. It takes time, creative thought, and persistent energy. Again, attitude is paramount. Go into the transformation of your schedule with the stubborn belief that every problem has its solution contained within it. Poke and push and tinker and putz around. Stay loose and do not get hooked on one way of looking at it — even if that way is something you spent years making, and it is just sooooo beautiful to you. A lot of wonderful cars have been created, some by Ford, some by GM, some by Chrysler. We thought they were so beautiful. Now we ride in Hondas.

8

THE WHOLE CURRICULUM

We enunciate two educational commandments,
"Do not teach too many subjects," and again
"What you teach, teach thoroughly."
—ALFRED NORTH WHITEHEAD

MORE IS LESS

The only thing more fragmented than the schedule is the curriculum behind it. Like two dead-end kids, it is hard to see which one is a worse influence on the other. We stick four to five "major" (math, English-reading, science, and social studies) and maybe four "minor" (PE, art, a language maybe, computer time) subjects into time slots and mix them all up. We add in half a dozen extraneous mini-courses of the Substance Abuse/Family Life type. Then we mix in three or four major holidays, several art displays, concerts, plays, talent shows, and poetry readings, all unconnected in any way to a central curricular thrust, theme, topic, or plan. Then during the year we sprinkle in a dozen more unrelated activities of the Mr. Wildlife Snake Assembly type. Not fully content with this melange, we toss in dozens of social events and videos and pizza parties. Then we preheat the staff, pop the whole thing into the schedule furnace, and stand back. Voila—a godawful mess. We call this mess our curriculum.

The need to make the curriculum more coherent and more whole is seen as one of the very most pressing issues in public education now. In and of itself, any one of the hundreds of distinct experiences students are involved with in the school year may be justifiable. Many of them might even be special. Taken together it becomes a classic case of more being less. When one objectively examines such a thing, one would have to assume that our two million teachers spend lonely weeks each summer desperately wondering what they can possibly do with the kids next year. Then by some miracle a thousand things descend from above

79

and the poor teachers' dilemma ends in a thundershower of absolutely unrelated activities, courses, experiences, studies, visitors, lectures, videos, audios, software, hardware, field trips, games, assemblies, adventures, textbooks, and worksheets ever more elaborately concealed in slicker and slicker colorized computer graphics.

Teachers have a far more difficult time deciding what *not* to do than what *to* do. As principal I had to virtually stand guard at the door to the school to keep "curriculum crammers" out: civic groups, national organizations, local councils, single-interest parents, the state department's mandate of the month, the calendar's holiday or emphasis of the month, supervisors with some hot new thing they picked up at a conference somewhere, travelling salesmen selling textbooks, agents trying to book juggling acts, and on and on.

A Message from Your Local Police

One day I received a formal notice from the State Superintendent himself. He noted in his memo that he had recently had lunch with the State Police Chief. What they ate was not mentioned. As a result of this extraordinary luncheon, however, every middle-level school in the state was to "Adopt a Local Police Officer." That police officer was to come into the school and visit for a class period with every single class. Twice a year, at least. Two or three full school assemblies and several evening presentations to parents would round it off nicely. This program would stimulate better relations between police and kids. Crime would lessen. The state would flourish. The world would soon be a much better place through this simple addition to our pathetic little school curriculum.

What did I do? What could I do? We already had excellent relations with the police. Our DARE officer—six three, blond, clear blue-eyed Jack Armstrong—was quite popular. We already had local, state, and federal mandates for programs on substance abuse, child abuse, family life, self-esteem, and Junior Achievement, not to mention bus safety, bicycle safety, recycling safety, and safety safety. About the only currently popular educational program we were not required to have was the distribution of free condoms.

I did the only intelligent thing under the circumstances—I shredded the memo. Just ignored it. I figured that if they were serious they would have to develop a monitoring system to ensure that all middle-level schools were in compliance. "Every constituency would have to be represented." That would take a committee of 200 teachers, principals, state officials, parents, students, taxpayers, citizens, illegal aliens, and police parachutists, statewide. It would also take hundreds of thousands of dollars, and it could take years to implement. If we ever *really* had to Adopt-a-Cop, we could always finesse it later.

As it turned out, the State Superintendent retired within a year, the Police Chief was reassigned, and that was the last we ever heard of this wondrous new program. Think of the bother that would have been caused if we had taken that memo seriously. The point is that *more is less*. Transforming a curriculum is a lot like cleaning an attic. To paraphrase Thoreau, "Every time you wish to keep something, throw two other things out instead."

The Politics of Culture

Any discussion of curriculum, of what will be taught, is political. In our look at teaching/learning we noted that separating the what from the how is inappropriate. By this standard then, discussion of teaching/ learning, as a broader framework for the often inappropriately separated topics of curriculum and instruction, is also political.

That is unfortunate. The overtly political tone and implications of the discussion cloud the issues and impede progress. In any era it is difficult to define precisely what students should learn and precisely how they should learn it. In our modern era the culture itself is in as great a flux as at any time in its history. When the information available and the technological means to review that information have increased phenomenally, it becomes even more difficult to make sound decisions here. In times such as these, we again see polarity. The traditionalists line up behind cultural literacy and content, and the progressives advocate multicultural diversity and process (Brandt, 1988). Again, dichotomy.

Again, balance is required. We need to move to greater acceptance of diversity, even while attempting to broaden understanding of our commonality. We need to state that content is important, that we do not study limericks with the intensity that we study Shakespeare, even while we emphasize that the study of limericks or Shakespeare has little merit if presented out of context, by dispirited teachers, in a dull manner, or in a way that demeans student intelligence.

In looking at issues of multiculturalism, of racial and gender diversity, we also need to take a balanced, fair view. It may be difficult to find great works of women and non-Europeans in art, literature, or philosophy prior to modern times. The search should be undertaken and the effort made, even if that means tediously uncovering texts or studying clearly lesser works at times. It is a mistake, however, to hold up works (anyone's works) that are not of great artistic merit in an effort to equate them with those of a Shakespeare, a Michelangelo, a Beethoven.

In a lecture I attended on this topic of multiculturalism, an admittedly feminist professor equated the work of Virginia Woolf with that of James Joyce. Woolf is a strong writer who wrote a few good books. Joyce is a great writer who wrote several classics. To say this is not sexism, it is reality. One could more legitimately argue the literary merits of Charlotte Bronte versus those of Thomas Hardy. To choose one or the other would then most likely be a matter of personal taste or minor critical consideration. To equate the "asexual," apolitical literary worth of Woolf with Joyce, however, is not good pedagogy, for it closes the minds of students on serious issues of cultural quality even while attempting to open those same minds on issues of social equality.

The larger issue is not simply to come up with women and non-European male artists of the past of equal value and stature of the acknowledged European male giants; it is to create a culture in which everyone has equal opportunity to attain that status now. This cannot be done in a culture that restricts the opportunity of those who, through no fault of their own, happen to have been born female or non-European. This cannot be done in a culture that suppresses or denigrates the accomplishments of its non-European and female artists. Nor should it be done at the expense of those great artists who, through no fault of their own, happen to have been born European and male. Teaching students to be discriminating is not the same as teaching them to be discriminatory.

Basics and Frills

This is another politically charged discussion. Who comes down on which side and when is not easily determined. It is best to take it off the battlefield anyway and simply accept that since the times of the Greeks at least, there has been broad, general acceptance of a balanced educational experience for students. Such an experience is one that strengthens mind, body, and spirit. At various times, under various presidential administrations, in various political climates, emphasis on one or the other may have been more or less pronounced. This is the military approach to education: left-right left-right left-right. In this century alone we have seen the Seven Cardinal Principles (left), Scientific Management (right), Progressivism (left), Admiral Rickover Replies and Sputnik Means More Math (right), Free Schools and Open Classrooms (left), A Nation at Risk (right), Cooperative Learning and Whole Language (left), Bush's Goals for 2000 (right). When seen in a larger context, virtually all of these programs have substantial merit. When taken as singular panaceas, they prove wasteful and counterproductive.

When the leftward policies arise mainly to make kids "feel good" and even turn over the process of education to the student—becoming student-centered at the expense of the teacher or parent—the result is murky, loose and potentially chaotic. Transformational middle-level schools have none of these elements.

When the rightward, "back to basics" movements rear up every generation, like recycled ad campaigns, and send teachers scrambling for "drill and kill" programs, the result is also destructive. At the expense of the whole being, such movements overemphasize the mental aspect of the student and often the lower mental properties at that.

We often get these reactionary movements in times of fiscal pressure. It is handy for school boards to cry "back to basics" when they really mean "cut costs." We often get *experimentalism* when there is more money around. Sound programs and sound policy reflect the balanced, thoughtful process involved in their development. Sound, balanced programs should not be subject to the whims of single-interest school board members or parents, nor to the vagaries of current political opinion. They are developed over time, through community consensus, and should serve as a base for future G/I. They should not be lavishly overfunded, nor should they be whipsawed in times of fiscal constraint.

Teaching/learning transformation need not be a matter of money, anyway. Primarily it is a matter of attitude, as are most of the other issues of school transformation. As in our earlier discussion of Teaming, teaching/learning transformation has more to do with distribution than production. It doesn't take additional money to integrate more art, drama, and music into the regular classroom teaching/learning experience. It doesn't cost a nickel for the sixth grade teacher to head out to the playground on a warm spring afternoon and play ball with the kids. We do not need more computer specialists when our teachers become co-learners with the students. It costs nothing to move from terminal teaching/learning to terminus teaching/learning.

In our schools science and history are considered "basic." Reading and math, totally basic. Spelling, basic, real basic. Who decides that spelling is sacrosanct, but poetry and drama—elements of literature, literature being one endpoint of spelling—are frills? One cannot do music without understanding arithmetical principles. One cannot do art without understanding geometric principles. Who decides that mathematics (our grandiose name for arithmetic in many cases) is sacrosanct, but art and music are not?

It is a truism to say that one's mind and body are not only inter-related, they are indistinguishably so. Who decides that active, antsy, growing adolescents should sit in one spot for hours each day, and physical education is a non-essential, a lesser subject? Who decides that students making things with their hands is less important than those students making sentences with their minds?

Art is not a "frill." Physical activity is not a frill. Manual arts is not a frill. Poetry and drama are not frills. Music is not a frill. All are essential in the development of a whole, healthy young person. All should be celebrated and incorporated into the regular experience of kids. Moreover, they are incorporated far more effectively when they come out of the curriculum, rather than act as adjuncts to it.

LESS IS MORE

We still have a long list. How do we winnow it down, where do we trim? The first thing is to cut that which does not *directly* promote the intellectual, physical, social, or spiritual well-being of students and staff. All the junk—outside assemblies of any but the first rank, top down curriculum that can be avoided, extra stuff like empty activity periods, prolonged holiday festivities, Friday afternoon video reward parties, hang-out times in the cafeteria, social issue programs (not current events), substance abuse overkill, etc.—should be cut. *These are frills*.

The second thing to cut is mini-courses, pull-out programs, and obscure, small enrollment electives. All of those compete with attempts to make the curriculum whole. *They are also frills.* What is more, they make it difficult to provide more of a common experience for all students.

In a nation ever more economically and socially polarized, it is essential for our schools to serve as a unifying force, providing equal and comparable educational opportunity for all students at the pre-college levels of schooling. We do not advocate identical experience, but we do advocate something far more similar than the socially and academically stratified programs currently in place in too many schools (please see Chapters 9 and 10). The virtue of such a "common curriculum" approach is extolled by many of our finest education thinkers, including Mortimer Adler (1984), John Goodlad, Ernest Boyer, and Ted Sizer.

The third trick is to take the good stuff left and, rather than cut, combine. When the schedule becomes more whole, when teachers work in teams with teams of students, the opportunity for interdisciplinary experience is multiplied. A whole approach to reading and writing across the curriculum is one example of this. Teaching "Reading" as a subject separate from language arts, let alone all the other disciplines, is a highly questionable practice. Offering remediation to weaker readers is one thing, and that too should be done in as whole a curricular context as possible. Running every student through regular classes in "Reading," even those who already read just fine, seems highly questionable as well.

When teachers have control of the Core time and are developing curriculum in concert with the arts and PE teachers, new patterns evolve. When major interdisciplinary units replace fragmented, single subject, text-driven approaches, there is more time and more focused, productive use of that time.

We now have the option of doing three to six major involvements per day, all possibly revolving around a theme or two (see Figure 8). This replaces the previous approach of doing eight to ten major-minor involvements, all unrelated. With a truly whole curriculum, the options are ever more limitless, and the schedule can evolve to reflect that. Students could spend whole days with one Core teacher, with perhaps one trip out to a non-Core area for work related to the Core theme. This, plus lunch and spirited physical play, would offer a workshop approach to teaching/learning that could become a wonderfully rich thing for us all. Let us take the top off our heads.

INTEGRATING CURRICULUM

Even though we no longer see curriculum as something separate from teaching/learning, for the sake of clarity for the reader we will address it in the traditional terminology. There is such intense interest in making the curriculum more whole that articles, practices, studies, and ideas abound. When we attempt curriculum integration, making the experience in the various disciplines more interdisciplinary, there are many avenues available.

In an excellent ASCD publication, *Interdisciplinary Curriculum: Design and Implementation*, editor Heidi Hayes Jacob presents a "continuum of options for content design." She notes a progression of designs along the continuum: from discipline-based, parallel disciplines, and multi-disciplinary, through interdisciplinary units/courses, and integrated day, to complete program.

Seeing development of a whole curriculum as a continuum is helpful in several ways. It demonstrates that simply relating a lesson in language arts to one in social studies is not too far along the continuum. It enables staff to see, however, that much of what they may be doing already has some interdisciplinary components. It takes pressure off the staff to assemble a complete program in order to feel that they are truly "interdisciplinary." Yet it always offers the promise of a truly complete, or whole, program as the logical end of a fully interdisciplinary progression.

I would add here that it is neither necessary nor realistic to expect that schools become totally whole programs in the sense that *everything* that happens each day is part of a larger, logical, identifiable whole. It may be all right to go out and play capture the flag some Friday afternoon without it being part of an interdisciplinary unit on the Civil War. Spontaneity and human interest in events of the moment always have a place in the transformational school. The central focus is a whole, related, continually meaningful one for students and staff, however. In such a fragmented realm as the modern American school we have a long way to go before we need to worry overmuch about becoming too holistic.

When we speak of integrated curriculum in the transformational middle-level school, we mean an experience that is shaped directly by the teaching staff for the benefit of their students. It is not a finished product from state or district offices, nor is it a compendium of textbook chapters. Both state/district guidelines and textbooks may have a strong place in the whole curriculum—but neither one drives it or constrains it. (Another excellent source here is Robin Fogarty's *How to Integrate the Curricula* from Skylight Publishing.)

A CURRICULUM DEVELOPMENT PROCESS

As with all other elements of the G/I process, time is essential. The same pattern seen previously in building teams (and to be shared later in Chapter 9) may be employed in building a whole curriculum.

What we did was *provide*

- information and research applicable to the benefits of a whole curriculum approach
- teacher travel to relevant conferences and workshops
- for one of our three annual school goals to reflect our work on interdisciplinary approaches for several years
- a team structure for teachers
- daily, weekly, monthly, and in-service planning/development time with emphasis on interdisciplinary unit development
- for this time to include team, entire school department, and grade level meetings
- an in-house form developed by teachers to guide and define the process
- continual administrative involvement in whole curriculum development

What we came to *expect* was

- sincere teacher consideration of interdisciplinary approaches
- leadership from TLs in the move to a more whole curriculum
- productive use of curriculum planning sessions
- major interdisciplinary projects from *all* students for our school and regional social studies and science fairs each year (We managed a phenomenal student participation rate of 94% at eighth grade, 98% at seventh, and 100% at sixth grade, with very few of the projects being insubstantial—and many winning regional awards.)
- a minor writing assignment (two to five pages) in each of the

Core disciplines each marking period, and a major one (five to twenty pages) in each discipline each year, to be evaluated primarily by the specific Core teacher, not just the language arts teacher

- development of interdisciplinary units by all teams for at least two marking periods the second year and all four marking periods the third year of the process (see Appendix for sample form)
- increasing horizontal and vertical integration of curriculum through continual teacher thought, dialogue, and creativity
- an increasingly whole, organic teaching/learning process/product

Definition of the Core

The Core normally consists of language arts, social studies, mathematics, and science. What emphasis these receive, how they are interwoven, and what additional disciplines are drawn into the web (please see Figure 8) is a matter of state and district guidelines, and school, grade, and team determinants. As we progress along the interdisciplinary continuum, it is increasingly important to pull other teachers and areas into the Core and to avoid going out for unrelated experiences. Through this progression, every class would eventually be a "Core" class, only with a different emphasis dependent on teacher talents and physical resources in a given room or work space.

The notion of enabling teams to maintain common focus, but with special emphases by adding an arts (fine, practical, or performing arts; music) teacher directly to that team for all or part of the year, is an intriguing one.

The Primary Colors Curriculum

We can change the lock-step progression of the year, as easily as the schedule. If we are looking for ways to study fewer things more fully, than we cannot cling to the notion that every student must have every subject every day. All sorts of rotational possibilities exist.

One that might prove useful is a model that divides the disciplines into three equal parts (Raebeck and Beegle, 1988). Known as *The Primary Colors Curriculum*, it offers three curricular strands interwoven with three interdisciplinary emphases for the three grades of the

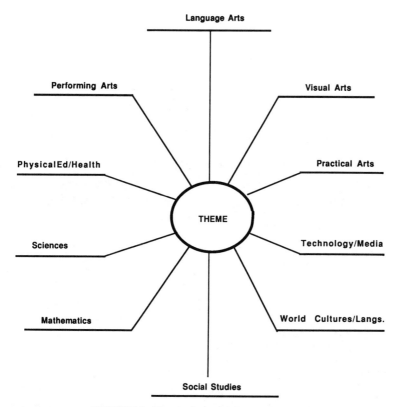

FIGURE 8. *Theme-Centered Curricular Web.*

school. Students experience each of the three Primary Color groups for one-third of the school year. There are several inclusive experiences that are placed between two color groups for the sake of interdisciplinary overlap, and there are integral experiences placed between all three color groups in order to maintain an even fuller interdisciplinary core at the center of the curriculum.

- *Red Group* (Mathematics/Science): mathematics, natural and physical science, health and fitness
- *Blue Group* (Language Arts/Fine Arts): modern literature, creative writing, speech, visual arts
- *Yellow Group* (History/Social Science): world, U.S. and local history, geography, civics, sociology, urban studies

Inclusive Experiences:

- Red/Blue: manual arts, performing arts
- Yellow/Red: architecture, economics, family life, psychology
- Blue/Yellow: foreign language, world cultures, biography, art history, great books, comparative religions

Central Core Experiences:

- ethics/philosophy
- aesthetics
- research
- technology/computers
- culture/communication (please see Figure 9)

Space does not permit going into further detail on the actual units created from the interdisciplinary, thematic approach of the Primary Colors Curriculum. Simply studying such a curricular web, in addition to Figure 8, may promote a fuller interdisciplinary awareness and experience. It is another map for staff to refer to when developing approaches that are more whole.

ENGAGEMENT: STUDENTS AND TEACHERS

A transformational school is one where inquiry is central. Thoughtfulness abounds in such a place. The teacher has moved from the role

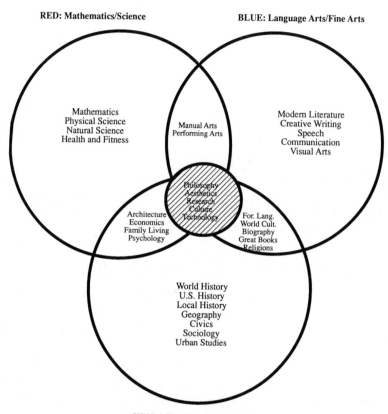

RED: Mathematics/Science

BLUE: Language Arts/Fine Arts

Mathematics
Physical Science
Natural Science
Health and Fitness

Manual Arts
Performing Arts

Modern Literature
Creative Writing
Speech
Communication
Visual Arts

Philosophy
Aesthetics
Research
Culture
Technology

Architecture
Economics
Family Living
Psychology

For. Lang.
World Cult.
Biography
Great Books
Religions

World History
U.S. History
Local History
Geography
Civics
Sociology
Urban Studies

YELLOW: History/Social Studies

FIGURE 9. *Primary Colors Curriculum Web: Disciplines.*

of all-knowing dispenser of information to expert co-learner. When the teacher does not know an answer to a student-posed question, that teacher does not ignore it or imply that questions such as this one are less significant. Instead, the teacher becomes student and finds the answer—or deputizes the interested student to do so. Everything is open to discussion, everyone is engaged in the pursuit of smaller or larger forms of truth.

In his latest work, *To Think*, the irrepressible Frank Smith says, "Schools should be fertile with questioning, not in the sense of teachers' constantly catechizing students to assess how much they know, but of *everyone's* (emphasis mine) investigating contemporary reality to try to understand why it is the way it is." Engagement means the people in the teaching/learning space are focused on something they all find meaningful.

It is a deceptive thing, this engagement. Highly motivated students can feign engagement in the most mundane activities. Twenty hands will shoot up to answer a low-level question of the "Who discovered America?" type. All heads will be lowered in serious thought during the 150 multiple choice answer exam. This may be evidence of competition for teacher recognition in the first example, for external reward in the second. It may be evidence of resignation with the tawdriness of the whole process, mixed with realization that this is the only game in town. Students will tolerate a lot in some circumstances. Tolerance and eyes up front is not the same as engagement. We continually remark on the adaptability and resiliency of kids, even while we take advantage of it.

Engagement is involvement in something that you will still be talking about at dinner time. It is involvement in something for several classes, for days, for weeks, even months. It is sharing your thought processes with peers and others. It is kaizen. It is joyful/rigorous pursuit of quality process/product.

We make a serious mistake when we buy the stereotypical myth that middle-level students "have short attention spans." Nonsense. Like all students, and all people, the length of their attention spans is directly related to their level of engagement. It is amazing how often in schools we do two things: (1) subject students to essentially boring experiences and (2) interrupt them during experiences they are fully engaged in to go do something else.

TECHNOLOGICAL TOOLS

New technologies enable us to make curriculum more interdisciplinary and more engaging. Once beyond the initial learning stage, computer experience should not be confined to a computer class or the computer lab. It is great to have a large lab in which all students in a group can work together. Along with that we need to bring more and more computers into the regular classroom spaces in a work station mode. Eventually many or all students will have their own computer terminals in many or all schools.

Computers do not replace teachers: they free teachers and students to individualize teaching/learning to a phenomenal degree. Time spent with computers is intensely interactive and productive, providing the proper software and teacher or peer guidance is available. A potential solution to the ever-present problem of ensuring the sequential teaching/learning of basic "3 R" skills in a creative, dynamic curriculum is offered by computerized scope and sequence skills packages.

One of the best of these is offered by Computer Curriculum Corporation of Palo Alto, CA. They provide a K–12 scope and sequence in mathematics, language arts, science, and social studies that is entirely individualized and self-paced. The format is colorful and engaging. In twenty minutes per day, every student in a school can develop and improve this range of essential skills. The time frame, the programs, and the one-to-one computer-student format combine to create a productive and engaging daily experience for kids. Such a process frees teachers and students from the repetitive, whole class teaching/learning of arithmetical and grammatical facts and enables them to move in broader and deeper directions. Although the teacher is still called upon to introduce concepts and monitor student progress, the more tedious elements are left to the computer to do, often in a far more effective manner than a single teacher can do anyhow.

Aside from the standard terminal and software, there now exists an array of interactive technologies that students and teachers can use in tremendously exciting, powerful new ways. Laser discs, laser printers, data bases, scanners, video and audio discs, Apple software such as Hyperstudio, Hypercard, Aldus Freehand, and Microsoft Windows are all available to transform media/information creation, retrieval, and processing into fantastic new forms.

(Note: the more time students and staff spend with high-intensity technology, the more we need to know of the safety of these processes. I believe we should know much more than we do before we allow students to spend large blocks of time in front of terminals, especially those capable of handling powerful high color and intensity programs, attractive as these may be.)

Curriculum development is difficult enough in single subject domains. It is a big deal to try to make things more interdisciplinary. It is also time well spent. Once teachers begin working collaboratively and understand the value of a whole curriculum approach, however, synergy goes to work, and the process/product can move quite effectively. When people are working professionally in areas of personal import, ideas rush to the fore, energy grows exponentially, and the outcome is highly beneficial.

Curriculum is flexible stuff. It must be open-ended and allow for teacher strengths, likes, and dislikes. There must be commonality without identicality. There is nothing wrong with one seventh grade Core teacher doing more math/science with outdoor biospheres, and another doing more math/science with computer biosystems, as long as all agree that the process/product is adequately achieving desired, shared student outcomes. (Please see Chapter 11 regarding an Outcomes development process.)

Curriculum is organic. Once it is written, it often gets stale. Use your unit forms, your documents, and your source materials as maps, not blueprints. Teachers create and improve curriculum constantly. Teams of teachers working collaboratively create and improve programs, and wonderful ones at that.

9
GRADING

*Democracy is based upon the conviction that there are
extraordinary possibilities in ordinary people.*
—HARRY EMERSON FOSDICK

The two issues of grading and grouping are inseparable. The manner
in which both are managed in the school directly reflects the ways in
which we, our students, and their parents perceive the larger purposes
of the teaching/learning experience. The disturbing and often absurd
ways in which grading and grouping are dealt with in so many of our
schools must first be understood, then somehow replaced by truly humane and far more productive methods.

In this chapter we will examine some of the practices and some of the
myths of the traditional grading process. Then we will look at specific
ways to make the evaluation process an effective, healthy, integral part
of the whole school. In the following chapter we will explain grouping
in detail and offer several ways to make this an equitable, productive,
and whole process as well.

LIFE IS NOT A BELL CURVE

During my first summer I looked over the prior year's computer
printouts of the student grades in our junior high school. A disturbing
pattern was revealed. Not only was there the startling incidence of failure mentioned earlier in this book (22% of all students received at least
one F for the year), but there was a comparable percentage of high success. Basically speaking, for every F there was an A, for every D there
was a B. The C's sat in the middle of what looked like a flatter version
of that notorious bell curve. Somehow the staff in the school had accepted the unproven and highly suspect notion that the student popula-

tion had essentially equal amounts of A, B, C, D, and F "intelligence." To those unquestioning teachers, the grades simply reflected the innate ability levels of their students. The phrase, "He is just a C student," was common.

Yet not all teachers were grading in this predictable pattern. Some had even greater failure rates, and several had far higher success rates. Upon further investigation I learned that those with the high success rates were teachers considered good ones by students, parents, and their peers. Those with low success rates were generally not well-regarded by anyone. My own class observations affirmed the popular view.

THE ANALOGY OF THE RESTAURANT

Imagine a board meeting at a large corporation in which the CEO is quite pleased to report the following: "One-fifth of our workforce is highly successful and productive and doing exciting, engaging, high-quality work. One-fifth of our workforce is basically successful and do-ing moderately interesting, good quality work. One-fifth of our work-force is modestly successful and doing average work. One-fifth of our workforce is relatively unsuccessful and doing poor quality work. The remaining fifth of our workforce is totally unsuccessful, failing ac-tually, and not doing much of anything." What might the reaction of the board and the stockholders be to such a report? Might they quickly begin the search for a new CEO?

Now let us look at another business, a restaurant. The maître d' reports to the owner: "Twenty percent of our customers love their din-ner and the service and will happily return soon. Twenty percent of our customers had a nice meal, proper assistance, and will return sometime. Twenty percent had an okay meal, okay service, and may or may not return to this restaurant. Twenty percent had a pretty bad meal, were treated rudely by the staff, and are unlikely to return." And what of the remaining twenty percent, the owner inquires? "Uh, half are in the emergency room suffering from food poisoning. The other half have been hospitalized for broken bones suffered at the hands of those two large and nasty waiters, Sir."

Whether we think in term of students as worker (corporation analogy) or student as client (restaurant analogy), the bell curve, rank-order mentality—with its subsequently skewed student success rate—is shown to be inadequate in dealing with live human beings possessing healthy bodies and active minds. We must move to the awareness that if virtually all children can learn, virtually all children will learn in sensitive and stimulating teaching/learning environments. If virtually all children are capable of learning, the grading and grouping patterns must reflect that.

RETENTION: A PLACE WHERE WE EXCEL

Americans have been quite good at retaining students in our schools. Retention is considered by the public and by many teachers to be a sound educational practice. The fact that there is no evidence that this is a sound practice, and strong evidence for the reverse is only now beginning to cloud the issue (Shepard and Smith, 1989).

No national figures are kept, and many states do not keep this data either. By examining the state figures available, and these include states from every region and socioeconomic range, it is estimated that we retain 5–7% of *all students annually*. First grade is the point of highest retention (20% in Arizona for instance), with kindergarten not far behind (10.5% in Florida). Of course in many districts it has often been far higher than this, with known figures of 50% kindergarten retention. Conversely, Japan and the United Kingdom *retain no one* in primary grades, and the median retention rate for all grades in Europe and the former Soviet Union is but 2%. It is nice to see that there is one area of public education where the U.S. is well in front of its peer group.

We know that student retention is associated with an increased probability of dropping out. Dropouts are five times more likely to have been retained once than high school graduates—and students who repeat two grades have a nearly 100% probability of dropping out. In addition to the great increase in dropout potential, repeating a grade actually worsens achievement levels in subsequent years (Shepard and Smith, 1989.) We cannot say for certain that promotion works (and without appropriate corrollary measures it will not lead to improved performance, even in the short term). We can say for certain that retention does not work, however.

GRADING SCALES: A MYTH OF OBJECTIVITY

Here is yet another practice that passes as appropriate but does not bear up well under scrutiny. There is little that is even remotely objective about a grading scale in a school, or even in an individual classroom. The scale is arbitrary and subjective. It is not statistically valid: it does not measure what it purports to, which is all requisite knowledge and abilities mastered by each student in that class during that time frame. It is not statistically reliable: it will not necessarily come up with the same objective results in other comparable populations over time. A school's grading scale is simply a set of numbers on a piece of paper. Individual scales that purportedly match the school scale are developed by teachers using different criteria, different instruments for evaluation, different attitudes toward evaluation, different teaching/learning methods, different grouping strategies, different materials, different sequence, etc. (Canady and Hotchkiss, 1990).

Another arbitrary component is the division of the points into grades at certain levels. Why is a 92 an A in some scales and a B in others? Why is a 68 a D in some scales and an F in others? Why is it that on a 70-is-passing scale, if a student masters 69% of something, he/she fails and must repeat the whole experience; yet if this student somehow obtains one single percentage point more, he/she may proceed right along the prescribed route with the same rights as the one who may have mastered 98% of that something?

How many of us personally know of situations in which a grade of 69.7 was rounded *down* to a 69 and a student failed English and repeated senior year of high school (as did a friend of mine), or an 89.8 was made an 89 and a student got a B instead of an A? This is done because, the proud teacher says, "They do not meet my standards." What about the international standards of arithmetic?

If these are such objective measures and standards, how is it that they vary from class to class, school to school, district to district, and state to state? Is it not so that teachers generally have a predetermined idea of how many kids will get A's, B's and so on, and simply set up their tests and grading patterns to assure that it occurs? Is not the practice of curving the grades after an exam an example of this? What about when virtually all kids, including the strongest students in the class, get an answer wrong due to their confusion over the question, but the teacher refuses to discount it?

Such attitudes reflect a distorted view of learning as some game that most students should not fare particularly well at. Such practices are no more objective than deciding students' physical fitness ranking based on who jumps the farthest—without taking factors of height, weight, age, strength, sex, jumping experience, and a host of others into account. Grading scales are an ineffectual waste of time and energy, placing emphasis on the wrong thing (Canady and Hotchkiss). Replacing them with unscaled, broader category letter grades based on teacher evaluation of performance and ability is a strong first step in development of a sound evaluation program.

To point up the flaws in grading scales is not to say that teachers are unable to evaluate student mastery. Freeing teachers from reliance on a grading scale may enable them to become far more thoughtful, truly critical, and helpful in their means of evaluation. Although I would personally prefer to dispense with grades altogether and move to narrative evaluations based on a full portfolio of student work and projects, there are ways to make the grading system far more beneficial than presently. I think that it is fair to say that most students who succeed to any degree in school do so as much in spite of our antiquated, subjective, and often inane, evaluation systems as they do because of them.

SUCCESS BREEDS SUCCESS

Returning to the notion of schools as humane businesses, it becomes totally unacceptable to have such low success rates in so many of our schools. The best businesses often operate with 98–99% success rates for their product performance and customer satisfaction. What percentage of Americans leave school feeling fulfilled intellectually, psychoemotionally, or otherwise? What percentage speak glowingly of their days in middle school, in high school? What percentage become readers, thinkers, makers, shapers, innovators, active citizens, lifelong learners? It is not close to 98%. Overall it may be closer to 25%, if that. Do the school practices reflect the natural patterns in the population, or do they perpetuate the unnatural disparities?

Success breeds success. This simple little nostrum can become a powerful slogan in a transformational school. It is a truism. It is a fact. Success breeds success. Say it often, establish evaluation practices accordingly. It has nothing to do with handing out worthless A's. We did not make it easier to get A's at our school. We made it a darn sight harder to get F's, though.

Accountability without Failure: Turning D's and F's into U's

We need accountability. Everywhere schools are being pounded for lack of accountability. I agree. Accountability does not equate to student failure, however. Accountability means that we are doing appropriate things to ensure that virtually all children learn, that we can measure what we are doing, and that we can explain and justify this to our clients – students, parents, and taxpayers.

Accountability is having report cards that are fully descriptive, that explain the grading philosophy and format, that offer a broad picture of school performance to the students and parents. Accountability is having a bottom line, but that line does not say "Failure," it says "Unacceptable."

Why have a D and an F as grading options? Are not both of those grades unacceptable? We simply collapsed the two categories into one category and called it just that, "Unacceptable." It was used to evaluate work that just did not measure up to what the student was capable of. We used A to signify work that was "Outstanding," B to signify work that was "Commendable," and C to signify work that was "Acceptable."

It is important to note here that any competent teacher can determine a student's capability quite accurately over time. Not in the first two or three weeks, however. This is one good reason for not grading students at all early in a school year. Diagnosing and evaluating, yes, grading and ranking, no.

My first week as principal I found a crumpled math paper on the floor in our eighth grade hall. It had a bright red 67 at the top. This was a discarded "gift" from the math teacher, who just happened to have the lowest student success rate of any teacher in the school. What are we doing to kids when we give them failing grades on the third day of the new school year?

Incompletes and Making up Work

We developed two other evaluation strategies. The first was greater use of Incompletes. Previously they could be given but had to be made up in the first three weeks of the next marking period. For a student far behind due to absence, trauma, or any other reason, this often proved discouraging and therefore counterproductive. We decided that I's could be carried over an entire course, provided they were made up by the end of that course, like in college. If they were not, they became U's.

We did not simply forget about the work, however. If it was considered important enough to be assigned, it was considered important enough to be completed. We provided many options to complete the work, as well. We had staff available during lunch and social time every day for kids to come in and do work. We called parents to engage their assistance and to determine why work was incomplete.

In a teaming structure there are many opportunities to take individuals or small groups aside to make up work, while the larger group is involved in something. We also provided a block of "down time" at the end of a marking period for students to make up work, while those who had finished participated in fun, large group activities. The extra support of the resource teachers on the teams, and the Learning Lab structure, also was highly beneficial in this process.

The best way to assure that work gets completed is to make certain that it is worth doing, that it is meaningful to the students, and that the perception of relevance is shared.

The CP: Conditional Pass

The second strategy was creation of the Conditional Pass, or CP. This gave teachers and students a safety valve in the rare case of a student who had not completed the coursework acceptably, but would clearly not be able to make up the work. An example of such a student was a boy who was perfectly capable and had always done fairly well in school until seventh grade. That year Wayne's mother developed a terminal cancer and he began missing great chunks of school. When he did come, he was distracted and depressed.

His mother died in the spring. Wayne did not show up for our required summer school to make up the several U's he had received. We determined that to fail him would do far more harm than good and that another year in seventh grade would likely end in his dropping out entirely. Wayne was given a CP in those three courses he had U's in; the reasons for that were explained to him and his father, and he began the next year with his peers in eighth grade. Wayne's academic performance was far better that year, and we all felt that our new flexibility had served everyone well.

When teachers become more grade sensitive and provide more and more support for students, making it hard for them to fail, the CP is not employed very often. Having teachers working in teams and able to discuss the grading of all their students each marking period is a tremendous assist to accountability in this regard. With the addition of student-teacher advisory and a CARE Committee, students are simply not going to fall through the cracks and go through even a marking period without teachers zeroing in on unacceptable work. With a flexible schedule and lower class loads, there is far more time for students to make up work in school and to obtain extra assistance during the school day. With students' affective needs being more fully met in the transformed school, there is far less incidence of negative classroom behavior that translates into lower grades in less effective schools.

Instant Eighth Graders

Now we are at a point where the practice of retention has been thoroughly discredited and shown to have no educational merit except in the most extreme circumstances. Yet in many school systems we have a glut of previously-retained kids, and they are not happy campers. This was definitely the case in our school system, and in our school.

Somehow it has never occurred to us to attempt to amend the educational fiasco of retaining kids without providing a different experience for them the second year. We decided that since the evidence shows that retained kids are far more likely to drop out, that twice-retained kids are almost certain to drop out, and that there is no law against accelerating previously-retained kids, we were going to try something new. Voila: Instant Eighth Graders.

As part of the CARE Committee work we continually identified and monitored CARE students. Most of them had been retained once, and several twice. Every once in a while we would find a kid who had been retained three times before getting to us. In defense of our district, those students had always come from somewhere else and entered our program during the middle-level years. What did it say about the sending district, however?

We looked at all factors involved. We talked at length to the student. We talked to the sending school if possible, while carefully reviewing all records. We talked to the parents or guardians. We talked among our own staff, guidance, support teachers, administrators. If it appeared worth the risk, we would accelerate the student. Simply plunk him/her right into a new grade setting if it was a transfer situation, or skip a grade if it was the beginning of the school year.

There are many potential benefits to this practice. There are a few potential shortcomings. On the plus side, you will often see a complete rebirth of motivation and commitment on the part of the student. Sometimes this happens instantaneously. You will almost invariably see a tremendous improvement in attitude and behavior. Generally we find that attendance improves significantly, and grades do as well. Most of the time parents are excited and pleased at the new opportunity and the new belief shown in their child. They feel much better about the school.

On the minus side, there is a chance that the move will feel overwhelming to the student. If the student's self-esteem is quite low, it will take a lot of encouragement from staff and home in the initial stages. If the student is presently a less-capable learner (though many retained kids are *not*), the academic pressures and possible curricular "holes" will prove daunting. Again, great support here is essential. Making the deal open-ended is helpful too. Allowing the student the option of returning to the lower grade can be a psychological safety net.

The Terror of Happy Hollow Elementary

When word was out that we were willing to accelerate kids, an elementary principal gave me a call. She was a solid administrator, traditional in her approach. And she had a problem. Juanita was twelve years old and in the fourth grade. Juanita was big and she was loud and she was rough. We already knew her older brother. He was at our school, on the CARE list, and somewhat inappropriately named Angel. He had a history of trouble at the elementary level, but we found him to be making terrific progress in our program. Perhaps he would even become angelic in time. Juanita, however, was having a terrible year.

The principal told me that Juanita was beating up little kids, hated her teacher, had gotten into several shouting matches with the principal, even pushed her once, and was being suspended regularly. Would we help?

The next week our staff, despite some trepidation, met Juanita and welcomed her to one of the sixth grade teams. She and her Spanish-speaking mother met her advisor (who was also one of her two Core teachers), her counselor, the assistant principal, and the Learning Lab teacher who would be working with her daily. Her mother was clearly happy with the prospect of change and a fresh start. They then took a long, slow tour of the building with a student guide. This was late October.

Juanita, the terror of Happy Hollow Elementary, did not receive a single discipline referral that year. She was not in a single fight; she had no problems with anyone. She smiled a lot, came to school on time every day, got solid grades in most subjects, and strong ones in a few. She fit right in socially and physically. She became a completely different person in the new setting. We saw similar patterns repeated many times with kids from twelve to fifteen years of age, boys and girls, all kinds of kids.

We accelerated previously-retained students in approximately twenty instances in two years. In all but two of those instances, the behavior and attitude of the student improved remarkably. In one instance there was no change: it stayed bad. In one instance it gradually got worse, although it may have deteriorated even if we had not made the change.

In terms of academic performance it is fair to say that virtually all of the students received better grades. Only three students, including the two behavior problem students above, did unacceptable work after being accelerated. The success of the students was at least in part due to the transformational school experience they were in vis-a-vis the ones they had previously attended. It is clear from our limited experience, however, that the practice of accelerating previously-retained students certainly will not hurt them in a proper, caring environment. I have seen it to be a powerful tool in reshaping a student's entire educational outlook. Try it.

Improvement Honor Roll

A fine way to provide additional incentive and recognition for the "born again" student is adding an *improvement* component to the typical honor roll. In a balanced school program, where student achievement is broad and can be celebrated without demeaning other students, there is a place for an Honor Roll. By creating an improvement category, we celebrate not only the achievement of those who excel, but also the effort of those who improve substantially.

We determined membership in the Improvement Honor Roll each marking period by looking at each student's overall grade picture. If there was a net gain of improvement in grades in two or more subjects, that student qualified for the Improvement Honor Roll. For example:

	1st Marking Period	2nd Marking Period
Language Arts	B	B
Social Studies	B	A
Science	B	C
Mathematics	B	A
Art	C	B
Physical Education	A	A

The student improved in three areas, and decreased in one. That would be a net gain of two subjects, and so place that person on the Improvement Honor Roll.

By having this Improvement Honor Roll, plus an All A Honor Roll, A–B Honor Roll, and B Average Honor Roll we encourage and recognize a far greater percentage of students than by just having an A or A–B Honor Roll. Yet we in no way diminish the efforts of the presently most-capable ones. We soon had over 60% of our students on one Honor Roll or another. Yet our percentage of kids on the A Honor Roll was no higher than it had ever been, and actually lower than the percentages at our district high school, a school which prided itself on its competitiveness.

A Whole-School Report Card

We value what we measure. Too many schools have wonderful philosophical statements stuck in a closet somewhere extolling the virtues of educating the whole child. Then they send home some little paper chit with six or eight lines on it and a number of grades opposite each subject. Perhaps there are computer-coded comments, perhaps not. At our junior high school we had just such a format. There was no order to the comments, however, so a report card in June might read as follows:

Jones, Joey   Eighth Grade

Math	C	English	D
SocStud	B	Science	C +
Health	B −	P.E.	C −

COMMENTS:

Inadequate homework
Misses class
Have a nice Christmas
Inadequate classwork
Have a nice summer

Now this might be a convenient way to communicate with a student and family. However, it is not a positive, open-ended, nor effective way. If we are truly about a whole-child approach in our school, our evaluation systems must reflect that. By incorporating all elements of growth and development that we feel to be essential, we are building a fuller picture of the student even as we encourage fuller development. If we want to see strong writing, higher level thinking, cooperation with others, verbal expression, and independent production, we need to evaluate these things.

The report card is the major personal communication vehicle from school to home. It is often the primary public relations vehicle as well. An effective reporting procedure emphasizes all that is important at school. It is positive and objective in its language. It is an opportunity for two-way communication, not merely one-way reporting. Like all whole school documents, it is organic and can be continually modified and improved.

BUILDING A STRONG REPORT CARD

First we agreed that our report card was inadequate in terms of student evaluation and public relations. We then assembled representatives from all teacher teams. We sent away to some reputable middle schools to see what they were doing. We looked at elementary and high school cards. Before we were done we had spent nearly a year developing a totally different report card. It turned out to be far more similar to the best elementary ones than to those generally used at secondary schools. We used it for a year, and then made further revisions to improve it. The result is depicted in Figure 10.

We offered something unique, a major departure from the earlier model. Parents liked it a great deal. The only criticism we occasionally heard was that, "It provides too much information." This seemed to be more a reaction to what had been than a criticism of what we now offered. So we took it as a compliment.

WINNERS, LOSERS, AND CHAMPIONS

As we learn to admit to the limitations of competition and to include the benefits of cooperation, we can move in healthy G/I directions that staff and community will both understand and support. We have just shared a number of ways that will enable a staff to turn the evaluation process to everyone's advantage. In the meantime we need to take a harder look at what we are doing. We need to break through some stubborn and nasty habits.

Think of a soccer coach who posts a losing record year after year, even while producing occasional individual all stars. After a loss she criticizes the officials, the players, complains about field conditions, but bristles at questions of her own judgement or competence. Whether she likes it or not, she is ultimately held accountable for the failure of her team to perform. It will not wash for her to claim that she just does not have the talent to win, that the kids are unmotivated, the parents do not come to games, the other staff members do not think soccer is important.

In the same district, in a school the same size, a coach produces a district championship nearly every year, and even wins the state title now and again. She maintains a superb level of success throughout the squad, not just at a few select positions. Her players appear on every all star team. Parents love the games. Even non-athletic staff see the value of what she teaches. When on that rare occasion the team loses, she does not blame anyone, not even herself. This was just not our day, she says. Next time we will probably do better.

Learning, Sharing, Growing, Caring

MIDDLE SCHOOL

STUDENT: _____
GRADE/TEAM: _____

TEACHER ADVISOR: _____
YEAR: _____

OUR EDUCATIONAL GOAL

To educate the whole person as fully as possible in 4 domains: the Intellectual, the Personal, the Social, and the Physical. All these are important and receive full emphasis in our program. We believe that every student can learn successfully and become a productive, positive life-long learner.

REPORT CARD

EXPLANATION OF GRADES:

O = Outstanding	A = Outstanding
S = Satisfactory	B = Commendable
N = Needs Improvement	C = Satisfactory
/ = Not Observed	I = Incomplete
or Not Applicable	U = Unacceptable
	CP = Conditional Pass

Note: A CP may be given when the staff determines the student is able to master work at grade level despite missing much school due to extenuating circumstances.
A U as a final grade requires summer school make-up.

OUR EVALUATION GOAL

We individualize evaluation by providing competitive, cooperative and autonomous learning experiences. Students work individually, in small groups and in larger teams. Achievement, Effort, Ability, Improvement and Citizenship are all considered in providing students and parents with as full an evaluation as possible.

CORE CURRICULUM: PERFORMANCE

Academic   **Personal/Social**

Language Arts/Social Studies   Teacher(s)
1 2 3 4   1 2 3 4

- Thinks creatively
- Communicates in writing
- Communicates in speaking
- Listens actively
- Is organized and efficient

- Is cooperative
- Is an active learner
- Is prepared and on time
- Works independently
- Works in groups

Reading Grade Level:
/ = begin year   X = end year
well above   above   on   below   well below

Mathematics/Science   Teacher(s)
1 2 3 4   1 2 3 4

- Thinks in depth
- Asks probing questions
- Performance on tests
- Produces quality work
- Completes assignments

- Is cooperative
- Is an active learner
- Is prepared and on time
- Works independently
- Works in groups

Mathematics Grade Level:
/ = begin year   X = end year
well above   above   on   below   well below

Physical Education/Health   Teacher(s)
1 2 3 4   1 2 3 4

- Development of motor skills
- Knowledge of health concepts
- Knowledge of safety procedures
- Values wellness behavior
- Knows and applies game rules

Physical Fitness Test Results:
Flexibility   Abdom. Strength   Mile   Pull-Up
FALL
SPRING

Fitness Grade Level:
/ = begin year   X = end year
well above   above   on   below   well below

GRADES

Core	1	2	3	4	Yr.	Electives/Exploratories	1	2	3	4	5
Language Arts											
Social Studies											
Mathematics											
Science											
Physical Ed./Health											
Resource											
Other:											

ELECTIVES: PERFORMANCE

1. _____   1 2 3 4 Yr.   2. _____   1 2 3 4 Yr.

- Is creative and resourceful
- Produces quality work
- Is developing new skills
- Is responsible and cooperative
- Understands concepts taught

ADVISOR'S ASSESSMENT OF STUDENT GROWTH

1 2 3 4 Yr.

Intellectual: _____   Social/Emotional: _____

OUR SCHOOL RULES

Respect People   Respect Property

FIGURE 10.

People are not identical, and students will never achieve at the exact same rate or in the exact same style. On the championship team the fast, rangy, midfielder passes well, and the big, tough, center fullback defends well. They are both fine athletes, in similar and in dissimilar ways. Both similarities and disparities are appreciated. The coach teaches, cares, and inspires. The team wins.

The grading issue is another bear. It too must be tackled head on. Eventually we may be able to create a system where we evaluate productivity through development of rigorous *and* humane standards of accountability without grading, ranking, retaining, sorting, or selecting kids. Many of us would be comfortable in such a system, and some of us have been. It is not likely that this will come about in many schools right away. It may quite possibly come about in time.

Meanwhile we must be thoughtful about what we are doing. Intelligence is not simply a matter of speed, nor is it a matter of style. Successful learning in a school is not the privilege of an elite few, or even of a large minority. If you have a brain, you automatically qualify as being able to use it. It is appropriate for a teaching staff to know that if the students are failing to learn, we are failing to teach. It really is that simple.

10

GROUPING FOR SUCCESS

Any system that does not form intelligent
people, whatever its other achievements,
is an inevitable social failure.
— *LUIS ALBERTO MACHADO*

As we observed in the preceding chapter, The Bell Curve is a convenient statistical method for ranking people based on performance of
a narrowly conceived task, such as an IQ test, an SAT, or on some
physical characteristic such as height or weight. Ranking along a bell
curve is not meant to determine one's innate ability, worth, or potential.
It merely identifies where one falls *if* one is to be ranked with others in
a peer group. When we fail to understand the severe limitation of such
a method and mistake the convenience of it for some greater value, we
misuse the method itself.

By accepting a rank-order approach to intelligence, we devalue virtually everyone other than the select few at the far right on the curve. It
is bad enough to be thought and labelled "average." To be placed lower
still is often traumatizing. This may result in the "seven-hour low-
achiever" syndrome—the student who functions perfectly well everywhere except at school.

THE GIFTED AND TALENTED CLUB

Those who have studied the phenomenon of human intelligence have
long known that it is not particularly quantifiable—that it manifests in
countless ways, including the artistic, musical, kinesthetic, spatial,
social, intuitive, and mathematical (Pearce, Gardner, 1987; Sternberg,
1985). What is more, we are constantly implored to incorporate a full
range of factors when looking at student ability and potential. That is
fine in theory, but numbers are so much simpler. So we persist in label-

111

ling our higher IQ kids GT (gifted and talented), though this title of superiority is usually based on nothing more incredible than strong verbal ability, often accompanied by strong parental pressure. For these kids on the far right of our handy bell curves we offer enhanced prestige and opportunity. This may come with unpleasant side effects though.

These kids too are separated and burdened with abstract labels and vague expectations of continuous exceptionality. They are also implicitly taught that they are better than the other kids. They receive special privileges, more interesting experiences, field trips, special status, unique pressures, and at an earlier and earlier age (Bray, 1979; Martin and Pavan, 1976).

This can be problematic if the percentage of students in a school labelled GT is 3–5%, which is equivalent to the national school age population estimates. But where is it that only 3–5% of the parents think their kids are gifted? What is happening in some high-powered school districts where we find as many as *30%* of the kids on the GT roles? (I know of an elementary school where *50%* qualify!) What is the point of labelling so many as "special"? They obviously are not special in that environment. They may even be the largest group. What of those not labelled GT when so many are? It magnifies their sense of inadequacy.

Singling out 15–30% of a population as more able than the others seems ill-advised at best. Set the IQ cutoff a few points higher, and suddenly 80% of the GT kids are GT no longer. Set it a few points lower, and voila, another boatload of the general population becomes GT overnight. A brilliant but anxious kid has a headache, messes up a question, and is not GT. Another kid just learned two of the test answers that morning. Yes: "Above Average" yesterday, "Gifted" today. The cutoff is 125 on the Stanford-Binet. You hit 125 you are in, hit 124 you are out. How scientific is all of this?

I am speaking as a person who was labelled GT and has children so labelled. Even as a middle schooler I found it strange that kids I enjoyed being with and found perfectly compatible both socially and intellectually were excluded from my academic classes. What is more, I had no higher percentage of friends and peers in those tracked classes, because many of them I found completely uninteresting socially and intellectually. What we all had in common was our IQ score, not a whole lot beyond that, necessarily: through this sorting, selecting process we may exact a terrible toll on the self-awareness, self-esteem, and subsequent performance of real human beings in our care.

Professional arguments for the benefits of gifted/talented education invariably come from those with vested interest in maintaining this specious status quo—supervisors, coordinators, and teachers of GT programs and the like. It is appropriate here to recognize that there is research that indicates higher academic success for gifted kids in homogeneous classes. Of course there is even more research that indicates *everyone* benefits academically from the kinds of classes established for GT kids: small size, motivated teacher, engaging curriculum, lots of resources, etc. (The work of Robert Slavin, and also of Paul George, is currently among the best in this area.)

What GT programs provide is enrichment. That should not be necessary in a transformational school because the experience should be plenty rich already, and for all. One way of resolving the issue in the meantime, however, might be by offering enrichment experiences in the program, either during the day or after school or both. These could be high-engagement, high-order thinking involvements, mini-courses, or whatever. They could be open to anyone based on interest. The truly gifted students would still be served through this process, but no one would be hurt one way or the other through the capricious labelling, pullout procedure. This could be called the *Additional Experience Option, or AEO.*

ENGAGEMENT FOR ALL

The tenets of GT education are nothing magical: they are simply the tenets of whole, engaging education—and they work for virtually all student populations, including LD students. It proves interesting to compare recommended strategies for LD students with GT students. They are often nearly identical. But the "average" kids in the middle get the worksheets, the rows, the desks, the same old same old.

To believe in not grouping students into GT programs based on IQ scores is not the same as believing that there are no intellectual differences in students, or that these differences should not be acknowledged and even celebrated. In any transformational school, *all* students must be engaged and fulfilled through daily experiences of high caliber. Academic achievement is to be recognized as fully as possible. We discussed this in Chapter 3.

In addition, we expand the opportunities for all students to succeed in every way, and in a quality school the academic domain is predominant. We do not lower standards, we *broaden* them. The goal is simply this—to have as many kids as possible doing as well as possible in as many areas of school life as possible. There is no reason to believe that the success of the less presently-capable student will undermine that of the more presently-capable one. Such outmoded thinking has no place in any public school.

GROUPING AND TRACKING

This is a point of confusion in the minds of many, especially the lay person. To many people it seems that tracking and grouping are the same thing. This is not so. *Tracking* is organizing all the students based on comparable academic ability/performance and then keeping them more or less together in these groups in classes all day long. *Grouping* is placing students together based on ability, performance, demographics or any other measure, but only for one or two classes. Often math and language arts/reading are classes grouped for ability.

It is important to note that tracking can easily result from grouping, however. In an intermediate school that I knew of, the students were grouped for math, language arts, and social studies, but not for science. Once you group for three academic subjects, you de facto group for the fourth in all but a very few students' schedules. This scenario was billed as grouping, but it was actually tracking.

This was apparent to me just by walking into a science class at that school. There was a noticeable homogeneity in the student population. I could feel a weak energy level and see that despite a strong and empathic effort from the teacher, the students were uniformly withdrawn and lacked confidence in their academic ability. I remarked on this afterward to the teacher. He told me that although they "didn't group for science, this is the result of the grouping in the three other major subjects."

In an urban high school in which I once worked as an administrator there were 40% non-Caucasian students (35% black), and there were 60% Caucasian. A visitor could determine the ability group level of the class simply by looking in the door: if the class was virtually all Causasian and preppily attired, it was an "Academic" group; if the class was a 2/3 Caucasian mix of prep and denim jackets and 1/3 black, it was a "General" group; and if it was 2/3 black and 1/3 Caucasian denim, it was a "Basic" level class. Although the school staff maintained that courses were self-selecting, virtually no students took classes from two different levels, nor were they encouraged to challenge the school's placement of them.

This looked to be appalling classism and overt racism. As I got to know individual students in the different tracks, I came to feel that what looked like classism and racism certainly was. I found several students who were placed in lower levels than they were capable of. They were generally black students. No one noticed that they were incorrectly placed, and no one did anything about it.

Even more disturbing is that this is not atypical in American public schools. Quite the contrary (Berliner, 1985; Oakes, 1981; Wilson and Schmits, 1978). Tracking has been with us a long time, and it is as well-entrenched as ever, despite the evidence against it (George, 1989; Oakes, 1986). Does this sound familiar?

GROUPING WITHOUT TRACKING

There are many knowledgeable educators who not only abhor tracking, but say that we should dispense with grouping altogether. They make a strong case for this (Adler, Berliner, Hammer, 1983). There are many others, however, including teachers, parents, and community members, who are not necessarily as knowledgeable, but are even more convinced of the opposing view. They adamantly voice the need to maintain systems that overtly track students.

In his insightful pamphlet, "What's the Truth about Tracking and Ability Grouping Really???" Paul George states, "Tracking has a tremendous hold in the public schools; it is unlikely that tracking will wither tomorrow or next year, in spite of the overwhelming amount of evidence against its use."

We believe in beginning where we are, learning from what works, and moving gracefully toward whole, pragmatic solutions to these gnawing issues. Therefore we do not have to create yet another either/or scenario. We can allow for, and even promote, individual differences in learning styles and abilities and achievements, without establishing exclusive little prep schools within our public school walls. We can effectively deal with this emotional, politically-charged issue by providing a balanced format.

The simplest and most productive way we know of for doing this is to group students by several means simultaneously:

(1) Group for differences in ability in math probably and language arts/reading possibly. Allow for overlapping in the groups.

(2) Make the groupings broader, with fewer divisions, rather than narrower with more divisions. Make the groupings broader in the lower grades, then progressively narrower, allowing for student self-selection, as students move into high school subjects such as foreign language and algebra.

(3) Regroup for all other subjects.

(4) Remember to denote the LD and SD students (see *Learning Lab* below) as another group in your diagram.

(5) Base grouping on a large number of factors, including preceding grade teacher recommendations, preceding years' performances, student desire, parent desire, recent standardized test scores, present counselor/administrator recommendation, present performance, and the logistical realities of scheduling and staffing. Do not base grouping on one or two criteria, and certainly *not on some standardized test score that may even be two or three years old*.

(6) Be extremely flexible publicly and privately with groupings.

Never pretend that we can exactly determine where any student belongs. Admit and explain the limitations of the system, and work with parents and students in individual cases.

A GROUPING PLAN THAT WORKS

With this in mind, and using achievement scores as *one* factor, not *the* factor, we can establish the following patterns.

Option One—Grouping for Math and LA/Reading

Math and Language Arts:

- Level 1 = 40% of students (achievement scores 50–99 percentile)
- Level 2 = 45% of students (achievement scores 30–70 percentile)
- Level 3 = 15% of students (LD, SD, scores in 5–50 percentile)

Science and Social Studies:

- Level X = Top half of Level 1, top half of Level 2, Top of 3
- Level Y = Second half of 1, second half of 2, second half of 3

(This "remixing" occurs in the second Core block of two classes.)

Achievement score ranges and percentage of LD/SD will vary based on the student population. Although not all students will be of equal ability in math and LA, most will be, and virtually all will fit into both groups when the groups are drawn this broadly. An additional group can be added in the higher grades, especially at the point where high school credit or prerequisite math courses, such as pre-algebra and algebra, are offered. This generally occurs in seventh and more so in eighth grade.

Option Two—Grouping for Math and Science

Math and Science:

- Level 1 = 40% of students (achievement scores 50–99 percentile)
- Level 2 = 45% of students (achievement scores 30–70 percentile)
- Level 3 = 15% of students (LD, SD, scores in 5–50 percentile)

Language Arts and Social Studies:

- Level X = Top half of Level 1, top half of Level 2, Top of 3
- Level Y = Second half of 1, second half of 2, second half of 3

(This "remixing" occurs in the second Core block of two classes.)

For Option Two to work, the LD/SD students who are taken out for small group teaching/learning would get that during the math or language arts time, depending on which is their weakest area. This is done so that only one Core block time is interfered with and so that those affected students would not have two periods of math or language arts.

It is inappropriate, even punitive, to give LD/SD kids more than one period of remedial work per day. In the most needy and extreme circumstances a student may benefit from two periods, especially if that student is unable to cope academically with even the general math and language arts programs. Of course we mentioned earlier that we encourage teachers to go into the regular classroom with LD/SD kids, as much as pull them out. The transformational school will evolve to a point where there are virtually no three-, four-, or five-period self-contained LD or ED students, and very few two-period self-contained ones either.

This Option Two scenario is advantageous to the degree that the Core curriculum is multi- or cross-disciplinary, with special emphases on math/science connections and language arts/social studies connections. By grouping this way, double periods can be provided in these more complementary areas in seventh and eighth grade. Due to the four-period length of the Core time in sixth grade, that can be done regardless of the grouping patterns there. The math/LA grouping puts greater emphasis on academic ability. The math/science grouping still provides for the tightest grouping in math and yet promotes the complementary aspect of the disciplines, as well.

If a Core is fully interdisciplinary and everything is interrelated, it may not matter at all what subject falls where. This is especially so when the subjects are no longer seen as sacrosanct, the boundaries become indistinct, and the time frames are no longer rigid.

These formats will ensure that the very strongest of the presently-capable students are not in Core classes with the very weakest of the presently less-capable students. Although actual school populations will vary, generally under this format there will be very few, if any, truly low-achievers with the highest achievers. This answers a prevalent concern held by some parents and teachers. Yet the format still provides all classes with a measure of diversity, all students in all full-size classes with positive role models, and all students with academically challenging experiences.

Small groups of students will be together in all Core classes under this format, when you group for one Core block of two classes and regroup for the second Core block of two classes. But they will not be in the same identifiable full class size group. And they will be intermingling with a variety of other students, both in the Core classes and in the exploratory/elective arts and physical education realms (please see Figure 11).

THE LEARNING LAB

Several times we have referred to the establishment of a Learning Lab. In the area of grouping, this program will utilize a proven method for supporting the presently less-capable student without slowing down

Grouping for Mathematics and Language Arts

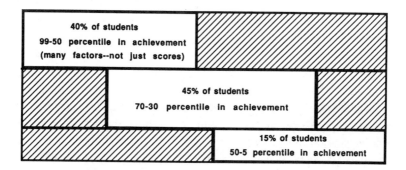

Grouping for Social Studies and Science

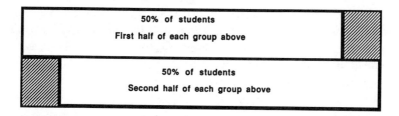

Note: Achievement ranges are based on many factors not simply standardized test scores. These ranges will of course vary in different student populations.

FIGURE 11. A Flexible Grouping Arrangement.

the others. This is a holistic program that works on several levels simultaneously. When this school feature is developed, myriad difficulties with grading, grouping, retention, and behavior are reduced drastically.

Earlier it was noted how we systematically eliminated Leper Colonies. One such process involved rethinking our approach to remedial reading classes. Previously the school had one Reading Specialist (whom we will call Ms. Felice) who taught five classes of about fifteen kids each, although they were never all there due to absence, discipline referrals, cutting, suspensions, etc. Nine or ten in attendance was far more likely. With that motley crew (several of whom actually wore vile Motley Crue tee-shirts, extolling their right to be failures and degenerates), Ms. Felice attempted to teach in a traditional square body/fat head style, all students doing approximately the same thing, generally pounding through elementary storybooks, often using the deadly-at-any-level-or-grade "round robin" reading approach, or pecking at worksheets. It wasn't working. Ms. Felice was as frustrated and bored as the kids, despite her deep commitment to them.

Over time, through her efforts and our support, a totally different experience evolved. We decided that "less is more." Seeing that we were not serving all the kids anyway, we cut to those most desperately in need. We got the LD kids off her roles entirely, as they were already receiving tutoring from their LD teachers. Instead we focused only on those we diagnosed as SD, or School Disabled. What is more, we went to class sizes of three to ten, with an assistant to help when there were more than five students in a class.

Then we took a new room and transformed it from the desk and dungeon format to something much more like a primary school classroom. Ms. Felice brought in plants she purchased herself and adorned the large room with them. She obtained bean bag cushions and used shelving to create a quiet reading corner. We got tables and chairs, computers, and bright new materials and posters. Now the space was varied and encouraged individual, one-to-one, pairs, small group or even whole group (though still small group) teaching/learning. Several different activities could now occur simultaneously without proving distracting to the students.

Ms. Felice also changed her teaching/learning approach. First she keyed what she was doing to what was happening in the teams from which her kids all came. Her role became far more that of a support person and a liaison for the classroom teachers, rather than an isolated "specialist." This enabled her students to build on what they were doing in Core classes, rather than taking on an entirely different assignment for this other class.

Ms. Felice began getting out to conferences and workshops. She rekindled her own interest in learning and expanded her knowledge base. This led to a greater understanding of a whole language approach as one way of enhancing her program. She maintained appropriate drill and practice, but placed it in a new setting, with different emphasis, used more flexibly.

The necessity of remediation was still essential for many of her students. Therefore every student had an individual IEP-type program. Together with her students she developed class rules based on our two school rules. By creating an entirely different, fresh, and positive atmosphere, remedial reading class became Learning Lab. It went from being one of the students' least favorite to one of their most favorite in the course of a year. The grim, black tee-shirts gradually disappeared, and discipline problems, even with those tough kids, disappeared too. Ms. Felice's referrals to our assistant principal decreased dramatically over a two-year span.

Our Learning Lab became a center of engagement and productivity that we especially liked to visit and to share with others when they visited. Ms. Felice developed her own colorful brochure describing the program in detail. She even went to state conferences to make presentations on the Learning Lab concept.

COOPERATIVE LEARNING: PROMISES AND PITFALLS

There is so much current information on Cooperative Learning (CL) that it is unnecessary to review it here. It is a terrific innovation, and it just may last. When utilized thoughtfully and thoroughly, CL has the power to do for a classroom what a whole-school approach to transformation can do for a school.

CL can be used in any ability group, although it was designed in part to eliminate the need for ability groups. CL places a range of learners in each group of three to four students, with a balance of learning styles and abilities as an essential component. It places responsibility on the teacher, the individuals, and the groups for accomplishing teaching/learning objectives, and in some instances for development of them as well. Different programs promote greater or lesser individual or group accountability, individual or group evaluation, individual or group assessment.

CL has many of the trappings of an educational fad. That is a great danger. With the way we typically operate in education, it is quite possible that CL will become so successful that it is universally adopted as the primary teaching/learning model. Then in five years or so, a study will appear that demonstrates that our students cooperate marvelously, but they no longer can perform independently or competitively. With that, we will rush "back to basics" and fish the old desks out from storage, and the old square body/fat head out from the trash bin.

Again, the key is balance. CL is offered as one alternative means for classrooms that are ineffectual and overly competitive. It is not considered by its originators to be the panacea American schools are looking for. There is a large place for formal, thoughtful, rigorous CL experiences in the transformational school. To see it as the be-all and the end-all takes us back into the traditional either/or trap.

We ought to look at CL in the context of the whole school. Installing Cooperative Learning is less important than creating a school where teaching/learning is cooperative.

If we group with pragmatic idealism in mind we can create successful scenarios for virtually all of our students. We can provide challenge and rigor to all, and yet not slow down the presently more-capable. Better still, we can offer them an opportunity to serve as leaders in a range of ability groupings, if that is their calling. Yet we do not prevent others from shining, from leading, from feeling that in some area they excel as well, or at least can feel fine about trying to.

More important than specific grouping patterns is fostering an attitude among staff that will then be emulated by students. The attitude is that although we have differences and we celebrate differences, the differences do not translate to net worth.

Being terrific in mathematics is wonderful. Being a fast and powerful reader is wonderful. So is being a thorough, solid contributor to group projects, and so is being the one who knows how to get the video disc running again. Being knowledgeable of local history is wonderful. Being kind and considerate to younger students is wonderful, so is being an accomplished thrower of pots, and so is being a fair and sensitive conflict manager. And being a clever poet is wonderful. And so is being a tough and resilient middleweight wrestler.

Being your best self and doing your best work are wonderful attributes that virtually all kids can learn. Healthy and productive grouping patterns are intrinsic to the mission of the transformational school. They enable all students to succeed, and none at the expense of any other.

11

GETTING THERE: ESTABLISHING THE GROWTH/IMPROVEMENT PROCESS

Every enterprise worth anything
has begun as an adventure.
—WILLIAM BUTLER YEATS

Transformation has to take place in a chunk. A whole-school approach requires total commitment, total immersion. We want to move, we want to grow, we want to improve, and we want to bring everyone along. We want to take great strides, but we are anxious that some will stumble, some will get hurt, some will abandon the effort, some might even try to discourage the most committed from going on.

One of the stalwarts of the middle school movement, Paul George, has, along with Warren Anderson, researched successful strategies for ensuring the longevity of sound middle school programs. They identify two categories of strategies, implementation and post-implementation.

The *maintenance strategies for implementation* include: participatory decision making, strong leadership and philosophical vision, taking advantage of the "window of opportunity," staff development, and evaluation and public relations.

The *maintenance strategies for post-implementation* include: awareness of vulnerability, maintaining central office support, networking with other effective middle-level educators, continued school improvement (our kaizen), state level support, and vigilance (George and Anderson, 1989).

These appear applicable to our experience. We dealt specifically with all of these implementation strategies to a greater or lesser degree. The method we used is detailed below and further defined in the One-Year G/I process shared in the Appendix of this text.

The post-implementation strategies identified were also largely applicable in our case. Those specifics are also detailed in the Three- and Five-Year G/I Processes outlined in the Appendix.

125

In Johnson City, New York, a model for transformation was developed by John Champlin, Superintendent, and his colleagues. Much of their work was centered around the Mastery Learning model of Benjamin Bloom (1973), and is outcomes-based districtwide. This widely heralded educational leader, Champlin, has defined seven critical factors inherent in transformation:

(1) The creation of a supporting, enabling environment
(2) The presence of clear, attainable goals, which are publicized and constantly in use
(3) The presence of a change agent who can effectively break the equilibrium holding an organization in place
(4) The use of a systematic, planned process that is open and subject to alteration
(5) The involvement of the community as an active partner and participant in any major change
(6) The presence of effective leadership with vision, a sense of mission, a goodly measure of courage, and a sense of the importance of followers
(7) A commitment to renewal that disallows compromising for lesser attainments and always aspires to higher levels of sophistication

We like all of these too.

FEW GOALS, CLEARLY DEFINED

All school systems have goals. Sometimes you have to dig around in the closets, but they have them. These goals tend to be numerous, they tend to be similar district to district, and they tend to be important, even lofty. They also tend to be universally ignored—unless an evaluation team is nearby.

This may be not so much because people do not believe in goals or do not like their particular ones. It is more likely that they had no part in developing the goals, they do not see the practicality of the goals, and/or they do not see the validity of the goals. The goals are not real to them.

In a transformational middle-level school there are several levels of goals. Each teacher develops two or three annual goals in concert with either a team leader or an administrator. Each team may spend time setting team goals. The school and the district have to have goals as well—both annual/specific ones and ongoing/broader ones.

With all of these goals there can be interference, overlap, and even conflicting ones. That is why the whole process must be thoughtful and thorough at each goal level. Ideally, all the goals at all the levels are congruent. This takes a strong, focused vision at the superintendent/board level and then throughout the entire system. When we analyze effective organizations we regularly find a shared vision, clearly articulated, fully embraced at all levels of the organization (Covey, 1989; Peters, 1988). It is rarely that way in the beginning, however.

The district goal-setting process can be similar to the building process and should complement that process. In this work we are concerned directly with the school, so we will look at an effective building-level goal-setting process.

In our situation, we already had a list of eleven broad goals drawn up several years previously by a district committee that only included five staff members. The list was similar to our state department's goals for all schools, and there was nothing wrong with any of them. The problem was the vagueness and the lack of full staff involvement. That list was not a working document. No one could tell you what was on it, and it was nowhere to be seen in the school offices, in classrooms, or on school forms.

We needed something real, personal, immediate—something of our own. So we spent solid staff time determining what our school goals were to be. This was a systematic process that consumed all of our staff meeting and in-service time during that period. An outline of this process is given below.

OUR SCHOOL GOAL-SETTING PROCESS

One week before meeting, all staff were provided with several articles extolling and explaining the goal-setting process. Teams were provided with current school goals, as well as copies of school goals from several other middle-level schools.

On an in-service morning we met as a full staff. We discussed the importance of goals and the goal-setting process in light of the reading we had done. We analyzed our goals as well as those of the other schools and came to consensus that the goals and the process used to obtain them really were inadequate. The fact that the individuals on that earlier committee were present and validated the inadequacy of that process was helpful here. We then realized that we wanted our goals to reflect teachers' beliefs regarding outcomes of learning and exit behaviors for our eighth graders. We had to determine what those outcomes and behaviors already were and what they ideally should be.

That same morning we divided into interdisciplinary groups of four to six people apiece. The physical education/health staff formed a group, and the arts staff formed a group. Special education teachers joined interdisciplinary teams. We began basic brainstorming sessions designed to focus on desired outcomes and exit behaviors. Therein we followed the rules for brainstorming that emphasize an open forum, initial acceptance, and recording of every idea, and no criticism of any. This generated many ideas quickly. A designated staff person recorded everything and was responsible for providing a list at the end of the session.

At our next meeting one week later, we asked the groups to attempt to define three to six broad categories to include their outcome items. Sure enough, all teams were able to do so. By the end of that after-school session we had half a dozen master lists, with every item placed in one category or another.

During weekly team meeting times we asked that teams write goals to define the several categories. By our next afternoon full staff meeting two weeks later, we had a master list of each team's goals statements and related outcomes. We then shared all of them, asking teams to look for ways to combine and streamline similar outcomes and goals language. Those amended lists were left with me.

I then spent time further synthesizing the data. In our next Teaching/Learning Committee meeting I presented the group representatives with an updated, streamlined version of several goal statements that included the best thinking of all the teams, with an eye toward incorporation of congruent elements. This version identified five goal categories: intellectual, social, psychoemotional, physical, and lifelong learning. It was critiqued by that group, then taken back to the teams for their analysis during the next week's team meeting time.

When the team reps returned the list to me with further modifications, I was able to draw up the goals in a manner that the full staff quickly ratified at the next general staff meeting. We obtained broad goals, yet with specific elements. Every single outcome previously identified could fit under one goal or another.

We had all benefited through the process. We had created our own five school goals (Figure 12), and we could fit them on the back of an attractive folder we developed for public relations purposes. They would complement our annual goals. This valuable, intensive process did not take us two years, or even one. It took but six weeks.

FROM BROAD GOALS TO ANNUAL GOALS TO INDIVIDUAL GOALS

The goals developed by the full staff through the above process steer the program over time. Each year it is important to focus on a *few* specific goals tailored to the current needs and interests of the staff and student body. I would recommend that no school have more than *three goals* for any year. What is more, it is perfectly all right to carry goals over from one year to the next in order to ensure that they will be fully met.

If a staff were to adopt moving to a truer middle school program as a goal, that goal might be sustained over several years. Additional and complementary goals might have to do with team building and advisory. Those three goals alone will keep a staff busy. Two of them might prove ample. Too many goals, inadequately pursued and too soon dropped, plague schools and discourage teachers. Annual goals should be thoughtfully developed with full staff representation and/or actual input in the process. Everyone should understand *what* the goals are, *why* they exist, *how* they were arrived at, and *where* they will lead.

It is helpful to revisit the broad goals and the annual goals periodically. We trotted them out at several staff meetings each year and asked staff to take time to reflect on how we were doing in meeting our stated objectives.

It is also helpful to base everything substantive done in staff meetings and in-service around the annual goals. It is frustrating and counterproductive to have Team Process as an annual goal and then spend precious in-service time on something such as Higher Order Thinking, valuable as that learning might be in another context.

Individual Staff Goals

Virtually all of the above thinking applies as well to the setting of individual goals for staff members. Those goals should be few, clear, and

OUR SCHOOL GOALS

Each student will develop individually appropriate:

1. **Academic** skills of reading, writing, listening, speaking, studying, computing and formulating, along with higher-level thinking skills of comparing, analyzing, synthesizing, envisioning, projecting and creating.

2. **Personal** qualities of self-esteem, physical and psychological wellness, and success in a full range of experience within a school that values every single person.

3. **Social** abilities demonstrating respect for, knowledge of, and responsibility to, the larger group at school, in society, and in the world community and its ecosystem.

4. **Self-expression** -- artistic, musical, dramatic, athletic, technical, manual, intellectual, and political--while deepening appreciation of the good and the beautiful in our natural and artificial environments.

5. **Love of learning** as a means of personal, professional, and societal improvement.

* * * * * * *

FIGURE 12. Our School Goals.

congruent and should complement the larger annual and ongoing school goals. One neat way for teachers to establish annual goals is to have one that is directly related to teaching/learning processes in the class and another that relates to professional development outside of the class — research, reading, writing, etc.

Powerful Staff Meetings

During one of my early years as a teacher, I served in a school where the staff meetings were held on the first Monday of the month, after school. During those forty-five-minute meetings, the principal stood behind a podium and talked or read to the staff in a soft monotone. Generally his topics were mundane policy issues. Sometimes toward the end of meeting he would attempt to speak to an educational matter. Although his ideas often struck me as sound ones, the delivery was woeful. Some of the teachers appeared to listen, some of the teachers read things, including newspapers, and more than one veteran teacher actually fell asleep.

The typical school staff meeting can be a grim experience. It is difficult for the principal to face all of those tired, and even jaded, teachers at the end of the work day. If that principal has little conviction and little to impart, it is worse still.

Depending on your pattern and history of full staff meetings, it will be more or less difficult to co-create something meaningful or even powerful at these meetings. It can be done, however. Here are some elements of powerful staff meetings:

- Begin with *Hey, Okay Awards* or something equally positive.
- Have *staff share* the best of what is occurring in school and at any conferences or workshops they have attended.
- Maintain a *professional, teaching/learning focus;* spend most time on staff development or broad issues of general import, least on administrivia that can be covered in notes or memos.
- *Vary the format.* Include videos, audios, music, readings, concise articles, etc.
- *Meet regularly*, at least once per month.
- *Meet at a most opportune time.* Avoid Monday afternoon. Tuesday is considered the most productive day, morning time is preferable to afternoon if that is feasible — athletic coaches are available then as well.

- *Have a set time frame*, and stick to that (fifty to eighty minutes).
- *Include all staff*, secretaries, custodians; try to let all school people share this powerful time together.
- *Welcome input on topics* and procedure from all staff.
- *Allow for the unexpected;* have a flexible agenda.
- *Have fun*, enjoy one another, create a festive atmosphere. Treats are great, too.

BUILDING CONSENSUS

Many decisions are made every day in a school. Most require decisiveness rather than discussion. When those making the decision are acting from a shared philosophical base, there may be less discussion still.

Larger decisions of policy and direction also must be made. For those decisions to be effective over time, for the organization to become and remain healthy, it is essential that consensus be established. This essential undertaking is also a complex and difficult one.

I would define consensus as *everyone being able to support the decision and the direction of the group*. It is not a matter of unconditional support, nor of unanimity of feeling. It is likely that on many issues of broad support there will still be a broad range of feeling and commitment. The long-term goal is full support from all on every major issue. In time, as the organization grows more robust, that is ever more plausible. Moving ahead consensually can, and should, occur long before that point is reached, however.

In our G/I process we struggled with this issue of consensus. We had a tremendous range of interest, energy, and commitment early on. Our situation mirrored the famous "Rule of Thirds." The Rule of Thirds states that one-third of the staff dig their heels in at the first whiff of change. I would call these the Diplodocus Third. One-third are in a wait-and-see mode. They are the Ground Hog Third. The remaining third are ready to take the toughest hill head-on—just waiting for the word—and no prisoners! These are the Rough Riders.

Those ascribing to the Rule of Thirds would say that you put most of your energy into the Ground Hogs because they are the swing group. You already have the Rough Riders, and you will never get the Diplodocuses. There is a lot of credence to this formula, though it may be a bit pat.

Another school of thought advocates the vacuum effect: push hard enough forward with the Rough Riders, and others will be sucked along in the draft. This is how Mile-a-Minute Murphy rode a bicycle 60 mph—behind a moving train in 1884. Another school would have everyone ready, everyone in sync before undertaking any significant maneuver. This strategy is noble, yet in some schools it could lead to group enrollment in the Diplodocus Rest Home long before it leads to transformation.

We do not have a clear answer here. The people involved need to use their best judgement. Moving forward under the assumption that everyone is part of the group and no one is expendable is certainly an appropriate jumping-off point. Trusting that there will be a natural attrition along the way is also important. In a three- or even five-year G/I process, many of the most difficult, resistant staff will actually retire, ask for transfers, take sabbaticals, leave teaching, or better still, become central office administrators. This can happen without a lot of acrimony. There is also the real chance that some will eventually embrace the changes, surprising others and themselves, and exhibit renewed energy and commitment.

Some elements of consensus building are

- providing everyone with lots of pertinent written information prior to a discussion
- building understanding and support among a range of informal leaders
- including strong resisters in individual and small group discussions early on to enable them to see the validity of the new approach, as well as to express the concerns of that segment of the staff
- moving slowly and thoroughly along a clear path
- encouraging, listening to, and responding positively to opposition as it occurs
- engaging in information-gathering and brainstorming type activities as a whole staff
- having staff members other than administrators report on and advocate a new approach
- bringing in outside experts to provide a different frame of reference and to demonstrate external support for the new approach

Once consensus is obtained, enact the new approach in a tentative manner. Offer it on a trial basis. Pilot things. Be certain that staff retain the power to rescind support if the approach or program is not successful after a fair test. And spend time during the initial stages of enactment reflecting on what is occurring and why, analyzing progress, strengthening the consensus, and so on.

I know of a university in which every new course is reviewed after three years, and either maintained or eliminated. With this continual review policy, staff members feel much more comfortable allowing new, even innovative, courses to enter the curriculum. There is a safety valve. If the course is not clearly effective, it will not remain in the program anyway. Consequently there is far less resistance to new approaches, but also much less likelihood of faddish courses outliving their usefulness and cluttering the curriculum indefinitely. A far stronger program is the result.

THE POWER OF RETREAT

A great way to move forward vast distances in a short time is to retreat. This is an extraordinary tool rarely utilized at the public school level. The reasons given generally have to do with time and money. There is no more efficient use of either than in a well-planned retreat experience.

Take as many as can go, as many as are up for it, as many as you can afford to. You could even ask for individual contributions, as we did for one weekend retreat to a mountain outdoor school. People were happy to spend $50 for the experience. Seek corporate sponsorship, tap the school board or the PTA, but go. Here is why.

Getting to a different setting frees up all kinds of time and energy. Doing different things in a different environment quickly breaks "role-freeze." People wear their blue jeans and their favorite hats, they eat and talk together, they hike and sightsee, they play and party together, they sleep in the same building, they see one another in new and fresh ways.

Determine the purposes of the retreat together. Create an agenda together. Plan both professional and social activities, and orchestrate a few surprises. Allow for a balance of structured and unstructured business time, allow for the unexpected to come forth. It will.

Prior to beginning our first year of interdisciplinary teams, we held a five-day workshop. The first day's activity was held in school and the second at a teacher's country home. The last three days and two nights were held at a wonderful old inn on a high bluff overlooking a grand river. During the time away, the group actually bonded. The power of this cannot be overstated. We returned in a state of energized joy that served us for many hard months afterward as we began the work of building a team-oriented program, where we had functioned primarily as individuals before.

Many teachers have a well-founded suspicion of staff development experiences. Too often they are led through exercises they have little control over, excercises with insufficient applicability to their classroom experience. My assistant and I felt clearly the staff's concern that the workshop time would be dominated by activities *the administrators* initiated, by study *the administrators* found essential, by things *the administrators* wished them to experience.

We were determined that this should not be the case. We hoped that with each passing session the teachers would exert increasing autonomy and leadership and that we would naturally relinquish direction and control. We felt it would be most beneficial if there was a gradual withdrawal of the administrators from the inner workings of the teams as the workshop progressed. This would indicate both our trust and their competence. In actuality the process worked so well it surpassed our expectations.

Eventually we came to serve more and more as assistants, even go-fers, when we were not participating alongside the teachers in large group activities. Our role was to keep the drinks fresh, run some errands, make sure the pencils were sharp. In fact, we came to realize that even when we simply stopped by to lean in and see how they were doing, it would slow them down and disrupt things, for questions would get directed to us, approval would be sought, and the synergistic rhythm they had created would dissolve. Before too long we left them alone for many hours at a time. We just sat on the porch and rocked.

FOSTERING A TOLERANCE FOR AMBIGUITY

An oft-quoted line of F. Scott Fitzgerald serves us well during the transformation process. He said, "The test of a first-rate intelligence is the ability to hold two opposed ideas in mind at the same time and still retain the ability to function."

When I was about eighteen, I was big into basketball and also learning something of Eastern philosophical thought for the first time. I noticed that an athlete in effective action had something akin to what I called "controlled looseness." This was the state you would enter when it was crystal clear exactly when to shoot and when to pass, and the hoop seemed to be glowing neon orange and about five feet in diameter. I found it difficult to obtain this state a couple of years previously, when my high school coach would literally scream at us from the sidelines, "RELAX!!!!!" He did not have controlled looseness, neither did we, and the results were as you might expect.

Now in some recent research on the brain the notion of "relaxed alertness" is mentioned as a desirable state of mind (Caine and Caine, 1991) for learning. To obtain this state the brain/being cannot be threatened, but it must be stimulated. This state of awareness is a difficult one for the non-transformed staff to comprehend. It is a state to advocate, however, in order to facilitate movement toward the flexibility and adaptability required in a transformational school.

It can be especially important to *foster a tolerance for ambiguity* when you are moving away from the lock-step approach to student discipline regulations and when you are developing interdisciplinary units that no one has ever tried before. This is true also when the principal proposes that a flexible schedule without bells will lead to greater order in the building, that eliminating detention will make the need for detention less likely, and that a teacher-student advisory will free teachers to do more intensive teaching, even as it requires more intensive relationships with students.

We return to the Yeats quote that begins this chapter. How wonderful it is to think of mere teaching in a school as some kind of noble adventure.

How incredible it is when grown adults, veteran educators say, "Aha—now I remember why I chose this as my profession. Now I know why education is not just my vocation, it is my calling. Now I know why I do this—why Monday is Wednesday is Friday is any day. Now I can say with some pride what it is I am feeling inside. Now I know why I am here, and happy to be."

Things are not always as they seem, are they?

12
LEADERSHIP

Imagination is a contagious disease.
—ALFRED NORTH WHITEHEAD

Why would we place the Leadership chapter at the end of a book about middle school transformation? It is not because leadership is the least important element. It is not that we subscribe to the notion that leadership is passe in an organization where people are highly motivated to succeed professionally and personally and realize that when they succeed so fully, the organization succeeds as well. Leadership is one of many concepts in our culture that is under renewed examination, that is thought to require fresh approaches. We study it at this place in our discussion because an understanding of everything that comes before infuses this exploration of what leadership is and can be.

VARIETIES OF LEADERSHIP

There is need for all manner of leadership in the transformational middle-level school. Teachers will assume official or unofficial leadership of the teaching teams. Committees require leadership to emerge in order to flourish. Parents can assume positions of leadership in many instances. There must be strong administrative leadership as well. As the school becomes more open, more healthy, and more whole, more people will demonstrate leadership in more areas. It is wonderful when virtually all staff and all students are taking leadership of one thing or another—and all are learning the benefits of positive followership as well.

STRONG CENTRAL LEADERSHIP AND DECENTRALIZATION

This is not easy to achieve, and it requires some of that tolerance for ambiguity again. We spoke earlier of the myriad decisions made in a school each day. These decisions fall into several broad categories. I would suggest first that there are many decisions and issues that the teaching staff want very little to do with. Certainly areas of school maintenance, bookkeeping, central record keeping, school budget, master schedule details, hall supervision, communication with central office, compliance with state education departments, and assigning bus routes fall into this category. Virtually all decisions here can be made by the administrative team with little input from the teaching staff.

Second of all, there are issues that the administrative staff would prefer to have little to do with. These might include daily teacher and team routine, classroom discipline, team schedule changes, the comings and goings of individual staff members, teacher supplies, individual and team budgets, and day-to-day matters of teaching/learning.

Third, there are issues in which virtually everyone has a large stake. These might be issues of student morale, curriculum, scheduling philosophy, parent and community relations, staff development, and grading/grouping policies.

The leadership of a transformational school functions differently in all three modes, with the underlying beliefs that (1) all staff are capable of using sound judgement and (2) decisions should be made as close to the point of action as possible. The first category above requires primarily administrative leadership and decision making. The second requires teacher leadership and decision making. The third requires consensus, with strong direction given to the process by appropriate administration and staff.

A fourth category of decisions involves emergencies or other situations that require quick, decisive action. Here, too, the matter is situational. If it is in a classroom, team area, or general space where there is no administrator present, the teachers act thoughtfully and decisively, with the understanding that the principal will support the action. If the situation relates to the whole school and the principal or an assistant is there, that person makes the call. The principal must be strong enough, visible enough, and respected enough to be able to act effectively in moments of crisis, with proper support from all, both during the event and afterwards.

A TRAP TO BE AVOIDED

As noted above, there are times when centralized decision making is appropriate. Leaders should avoid giving staff members the idea that they are central to a decision-making process when they really are not. When a committee is formed, everyone involved ought to be explicitly aware as to that committee's function and authority. The leader does not solicit the opinion of staff without them knowing to what extent their view will affect the decision. If the leader does not intend to take others' opinions to heart, that leader must not set up some "democratic" exercise in futility. It will ultimately prove worse for the leader-staff relationship than simple unilateral control. That is bad enough already.

THE PRINCIPAL AS LEADER: THE DOWNSIDE

Being a principal in any public school is an extraordinarily difficult and complex task. Being an effective principal may be impossible in the long term. For reasons too involved to go into here, the fact is that there are very few principals who become highly effective and remain so in the same building for more than a few years. The responsibilities are awesome. The constituency is vast and to a degree insatiable. The requisite knowledge base is forbidding. The politics are dangerous. The pressure is enormous.

With all of this comes long hours, endless regulations, a phenomenal paper load, little positive feedback, and mediocre pay—pay that is often less than teaching pay when the hours are computed, and no bonus for the great responsibility, either. That is the downside, a significant downside.

Then we look at prevalent leadership styles. Our accepted leadership styles in schools are often as outmoded and ineffectual as the traditional scheduling, discipline, and grading procedures (Champlin, 1987; Goodlad, 1983). We have many shell shocked principals who hide in their offices, not sure what they should do. Others schedule so many meetings in their offices that we do not see them either; not in the hallways, the classrooms, at bus time, or in the cafeteria. We also have the hard chargers ("I'll shock those shells before they shock me!") who get around quite a bit, yet leave anxiety and confusion in their wake. They know exactly what they are doing but are not sensitive or concerned enough about what everyone else knows and sees.

THE PRINCIPAL AS LEADER: THE UPSIDE

There is an upside to the principalship, however—both the position and the style. There are many fine, professional, focused women and men who do things well and love the better part of it (Sheive and Schoenheit, 1987; Smith and Andrews, 1989). They value and respect their staffs and are valued and respected in turn. They are tough, but not hard. They are knowledgeable, but not pedantic. They are hard-working, but not workaholics. They are compassionate without being melodramatic. They espouse an imaginative vision without being demagogues. They have learned to do what Thomas Pynchon advocated in the novel *V.*: "Keep cool, but care."

In his fine work, *The Quality School*, William Glasser describes the needed transformational shift from coercive, ultimately ineffectual "boss-management" to facilitative, cooperative, ultimately valuable "lead-management" (Glasser, 1990). This is similar to what the teacher/learner exemplifies in the terminus style classroom. The transformational principal models the desirable modus operandi in the school.

PRINCIPAL AS VISIONARY

What do we value? Why do we do this thing called school? How do we remain thoughtful and focused? The balanced, inspirational leadership style is in large part one of modelling. These are some of the things modelled:

- *life-long learning*—reading, researching, exploring new methodologies, travelling to workshops and other schools, drawing for inspiration from other realms such as art, music, philosophy, psychology, drama, and film, and sharing that with staff
- *compassion*—always trying to see the person beneath the problem, allowing for human foibles, cutting deals and making exceptions for people, respecting hurt, taking time to listen to staff and student stories of doubt, loneliness, fear, divorce, deprivation, abuse, anger, and unrequited dreams
- *saying yes*—to the teacher's missing half a day to see her child in

a kindergarten play, to the student who has to leave five minutes early each day to pick up a little brother, to adding one more person to the list even though the deadline passed, to second, third and fourth chances, to hanging art in the hallways even though the fierce fire marshall forbids it

- *being an umbrella* — for staff who are struggling with an angry parent, for the sleepless first year teacher who can't get it together, for the assistant principal who makes a poor decision in a discipline case and it backfires, for the secretary who does not type particularly well but makes up for it in other ways
- *taking risks and encouraging mistakes* — by supporting a teacher curriculum pilot project that is well-intentioned although not well-planned, by changing the schedule in a way no one has ever thought of, let alone attempted, by encouraging the basketball coach to play all the kids, even if that means losing some games
- *being flexible and fluid* — not getting stuck on decisions, considering every situation as temporary and every system as organic, making exceptions even to the very few, very flexible rules
- *demanding exceptionality while relinquishing control* — expecting only that staff are great but not burdening them with formulas for obtaining that greatness, letting go of time tables and fixed images of teaching just as we ask teachers and parents to let go of fixed images of intelligence and student success
- *exemplifying and exacting high standards* — bringing culture into the school, looking sharp, speaking well, noticing the details, expecting quality in every single thing that each of us does, never putting the words "good" and "enough" together
- *holding out the vision* — saying it over and over in a hundred different ways: "This is what we value, these are our goals, this is what we believe in," and demonstrating commitment in another hundred ways by thinking, observing, sharing, speaking, listening, laughing, recognizing, supporting, pushing, pulling, living the dream, being there
- *picking up tiny bits of paper* — seeing the totality, the macrocosm in the microcosm, saying "Hi" to the custodian slipping silently past, keeping a neat attractive work space, scooping the cigarette butt on the front steps, getting your hands dirty, keeping one eye on the earth and one eye on the stars

BECOMING OUR OWN LEADERS

Such a leader is distinctive, different from what we are used to. Such a leader often acts in ways opposite to the image of leadership many of us are comfortable with. Such a leader asks others to assume more and more of the responsibility for their own behavior, asks them in effect to gradually *become their own leaders*.

Modelling such behavior is extremely difficult for a principal. Acceptance of such behavior will be equally difficult for staff for quite some time. In *The Different Drum: Community Making and Peace*, Scott Peck says, "To lead people into community a true leader must discourage their dependency, and there may be no way to do this but to refuse to lead." In the early stages of transformation this will cause much confusion, doubt, and even anger.

WHAT OF FALLEN ANGELS?

There is no way that a school can experience a transformational process without some heavy resistance. Many proud and even competent teachers and administrators simply do not believe that what we are doing is all that ineffectual, or that a systematic G/I process will make all that much difference. Some parents and community members will cling stubbornly to their local school as the last bastion of stability and sameness in an ever more frightening world of ceaseless change that they cannot understand or control.

Beyond those two groups may be a third one of truly angry, disaffected people who will subvert anyone or anything that threatens their status quo, or appears to impugn it by offering something else. Peck calls these the "militantly ignorant." All have to be dealt with to some degree.

PRUNING THE TREE

This is an extremely delicate issue. We must always act on the belief that everyone is capable of becoming more, that everyone is accepted and everyone inherently wants to be positive and strong. This is the unconstrained worldview that we hold. Occasionally we are tested by truly disastrous forces, however. Sometimes it is better to confront such a force, such a person, than to continually attempt to cooperate. Alongside all the powerfully positive actions we intentionally make in the transformation process, there may also be a place for intense confrontation.

Such an approach may not be found in the textbook. There may be a few people in the school who are hurting kids, who are destructive in their behavior, who consciously undermine the genuine efforts to grow being made by those around them. These few people need to be appraised of the impact of their behavior—and its unacceptability. Just as we need to have a bottom line for the incorrigible student, so we need to have a bottom line of accountability for the damaging staff member. We owe this to our schools and also to the profession at large. As a profession we have long been criticized (and rightfully so) for our pathetic inability to monitor our own ranks.

FEAR IN THE FOREST

What we must also realize, however, is that even a "successful" confrontation with a clearly ineffectual staff member, resulting in that person's leaving, sends a shock wave through the school. Many members of a veteran staff who are unused to change, unused to dealing with personnel problems, will have trouble accepting the loss of a colleague, even an incompetent one. The less secure may begin to wonder who is next, who is on the imagined "list."

In our process, no tenured person was dismissed, yet the staff saw more personnel change than they had in years. This was accomplished through retirements, voluntary transfers, and non-renewal of two probationary teachers who were ineffectual. Dealing directly with staff regarding their professional shortcomings is a hard thing to do. Non-renewal is especially hard. If a veteran teacher hired from another program turns out to be far less than was expected, just how smart is it to grant that person continuing contract status and saddle a school district with a mediocre teacher for the rest of that person's career?

Once the replacements arrived, the change was widely seen as a change for the better. This was an opportunity for the number-nine-hitter-replaced-by-a-number-four-hitter staff upgrade scenario mentioned in Chapter 5. We took full advantage of the opportunity and brought in dynamic, exceptional teachers. But even so, this did not sit well with some people. Is it possible to create a great program, but not upset or even lose anyone along the way? I am not sure. I believe it is a risk worth taking in extreme cases, however.

COMPASSIONATE DETACHMENT

It is terribly hard to replace staff in a positive way. It is hard even though the end results will very likely be positive for the school—a stronger staff results, *and* for the individuals who leave—dysfunctional people are rarely, if ever, happy doing what they are doing. They often need a boost to move their lives in a healthier direction. It is beneficial to be as calm, as detached, and as compassionate as possible during such a procedure. This is terribly difficult for a principal. I was not always as cool in these situations as I would have liked. The process itself, however, is essential if we are to co-create the kind of school programs that will deservedly earn public support and serve students well for years to come.

POWERFUL PARENTS

All of us know the line often offered by school staff: "The parents want this to stay the way it is; they will not accept a change." When we ask the speaker to be more specific, to cite the study, show the data substantiating this broad and compelling statement, the person is unable to produce anything. That is irrelevant, however, because the speaker knows, and we know, that "the parents" referred to are *not all* the parents, not by any stretch of the imagination. But they very well might be a good percentage of the parents who "matter the most" in that school district.

We would maintain that "the parents" are generally a quite small, however vocal, minority. These people are invariably well-educated, yet they are often militantly ignorant when it comes to education and may hold to a severely constrained worldview as well. Their priority is getting their children into as prestigious a college as possible. They are not particularly interested in educational theory, in cooperative process, in humane practices, or in all students being successful. Often they secretly fear that the more success other children have, the less success their children will have. These people are often the staunchest proponents of tracking, of grouping into myriad ability levels, of gifted and talented programs, of lots of homework and tests and grades, of quiet classrooms full of kids in rows competing against each other.

There are several ways to deal with this faction. Listening, sharing, taking them with you on visits, inviting them into the school and its classrooms, and including them on committees and in serious discussions are all important. The best way to answer this faction is to produce (1) test results that demonstrate changes in your program are not leading to lowering of achievement, and (2) surveys of the entire parent body demonstrating clearly that this group is in fact a small minority, that most parents want a balanced, happy, successful experience for their kids.

The vocal minority places great value on "objectivity" and therefore will have trouble arguing with hard data. Patience, sharing, invitations, public relations, all manner of efforts to include them, listen to them, and allow them the right to their views are essential. We do not demean these attempts. Do not expect it to be easy, however. The thing to remember is that in time all but the most vituperative will ease up, realizing finally that middle-level transformation is not the end of Western civilization as we now know it.

WE WANT EVERYONE ON BOARD

We want everyone on the train. We start with this premise and we cling to it. If we are asking parents to support a new program, we must include them, listen to them, and tolerate even the strongest criticism in an effort to learn from it. If we are asking staff to make the commitment to every single one of their students, then we need to do the same thing with commitment to one another. It is appropriate here not to get stuck on those who do not come along, for whatever reason. At one level they make a choice. It is also appropriate to recall and emphasize all the successes with community, with kids, and with staff—all the personal transformations that are reflected in the school transformation.

EATING THE SAME FOOD

It is equally important to recognize the motivation of the transformational leader. Such a person is totally committed; such a person is excited about work virtually every day; such a person is not concerned about anything other than the overall health of the school. Such a person has an image of that healthy school ever in mind (Sheive and Schoenheit, 1987). Look at the actions, look at the results. Are they congruent? Do they sustain G/I? Do they further transformation?

Such a person is also sensitive to power and the symbols associated with its abuse. The transformational leader does not have a designated parking space next to the front entrance. That person does not separate him or herself from staff unnecessarily, does not avoid school dances, the cafeteria, unpleasant parents, or the student restrooms. The transformational leader is in the trenches, eating the same food.

This is not to say that cultivating a certain style or maintaining a certain seriousness of purpose, dressing well, or having a nice work space are incongruent with transformational values. Those behaviors can stimulate staff, they can model professional behaviors sometimes woefully lacking in a school. Individual styles are not nearly as important as credibility and integrity, however. These one cannot manufacture.

THE EMPTY BOAT

There is a wonderful little story attributed to Chuang Tzu, our ancient Chinese gentleman friend (Merton, 1965). Therein he describes what happens when a man is crossing a river and an empty boat collides with his own skiff. Although he is a bad-tempered man, he will not become angry in such a circumstance. If there happens to be a person in the other boat, however, he will shout at him, threaten, even begin cursing. All this, says Chuang, because there is someone in the boat. If it were empty, no shouting, no anger. He goes on to say, "If you can empty your own boat crossing the river of the world, no one will oppose you, no one will seek to harm you." Then Chuang adds, "The straight tree is the first to be cut down, the spring of clear water the first to be drained dry."

In our culture of self-service and competition, where we may

THE EMPTY BOAT 147

secretly dream of our own personal feature article in *People*, it is difficult to reconcile this voice from the past. We are more likely to feel that if we do not row aggressively, we will be bashed and beaten by a thousand boats more powerful, more successful than ours. As one who has grown up playing competitive sports, reaching for scholastic and professional honors, being acutely aware of ranking, measurement, wins, losses, and draws my whole life, I have struggled to understand what Chuang is saying.

There have been many times when I have gotten upset, or angry, been knocked off of my center, or even ran over a teammate on the way to the goal. Are we not all teammates, really?

Stephen Covey espouses such a view when he talks about the value of service, of doing what is right for its own sake. Tom Peters has identified the ethic of integrity that undergirds many of our most successful corporations. It is not either/or. We can act with pragmatic idealism, we can serve the school, the individuals, and our own best interests all at the same time. Over and over I have seen that insisting that themes of service, of integrity, of compassion, and of love for one's fellows supersede our lesser agendas is not only the *right* thing to do, but also the *most successful* in the long term.

Remember what Peck said about perceptions of transformational leadership. Others may not understand. Others may feel lost or let down in the early stages. Still others will never understand the motivation of one who seeks only to serve. For of this person Chuang says,

> To all appearances he is a fool.
> His steps leave no trace. He has no power.
> He achieves nothing, has no reputation.
> Since he judges no one
> No one judges him.
> Such is the perfect man
> His boat is empty.

AFTERWORD

*What is now prov'd, was
once only imagin'd.*
—WILLIAM BLAKE

This is not a battle we are engaged in; it is not a war. Too often we feel it necessary to add elements of cosmic proportion in order to give credence to our struggles down here in the fields and marshes.

Yes, what we are doing is important. Of course the mere mention of children, their minds, their realities, and their futures will stir the hearts of many, if only for the time it takes to read an article or a book.

What we are about is making it better—not condemning everything that is, not posing fantastical solutions, not selling neat formulas in slick packages. We are just about making it better.

If we are going to continue this public school experiment, there are a few things we can improve on. There is a genuine danger that this society will become so polarized economically, politically, and racially that we actually become unwilling or unable to send all children to school. In such a dystopia, education would be left up to whatever market forces create. Rich kids will get schooling pretty close to what they have now. Poor kids will get buried even deeper than they are now. Neither will thrive. Neither will have the kind of educational experience that is available right now.

Where is it, then?

I have long been intrigued with the notion of parallel time, or even parallel realities. I think that perhaps thoughts work in the same way. Why is it that in the same school, with the same kids, the same curriculum, and the same resources, one class of teacher and students is having a marvelous time, while right next door another group is enduring a daily dose of hell?

How do you explain that we took a school that was close to the edge,

149

that was full of angry, even dangerous kids, and frustrated, tired teachers, and transformed it in less than three years to a place of warmth, fun, excitement, and success for virtually all students and staff? It is not money. It is not political agendas. It has nothing to do with national testing or lack of national testing. It does not require vouchers or a change in the leadership of the U.S. Department of Education. It has very little to do with any of that.

It has to do with courage. It has to do with commitment. It has to do with passion and compassion. It has to do with community. It has more to do with spirit than with finance, more to do with people than with policy, more to do with attitude than with technique.

We have the schools we want.

When we want to transform more of them into places of creativity, joy, excitement, quality, and spirit, we will. When enough of us want schools to serve our children on more genuine, more whole levels of intellectual vigor, of physical exuberance, of emotional depth, of social compassion, we will have such schools. When enough of us come to understand that deeper engagement in fewer things is far better than flopping around "covering material" because "it's on the test," we will move to higher ground. When enough of us admit publicly that in a person's life love, or its lack, is generally a more powerful force than our SAT scores, our schools will mirror that sensibility.

There is a natural phenomenon known as "critical mass" discussed in a book by Ken Keyes called, *The Hundredth Monkey*. Apparently when enough members of a group or species come to a certain point of development, amazing kinds of awarenesses appear, and these often transcend natural boundaries. It was observed that in a group of monkeys on an island near Japan one monkey began washing his sweet potatoes a certain way in the salt water. Soon all the monkeys mimicked the behavior and began washing their sweet potatoes this way. When a given number of monkeys began doing this, at the same time hundreds of miles away another group of monkeys began doing the same thing. This is not particularly explicable. But it may indicate that when a group is ready for the next stage of development, they just go for it, independent of a lot of other factors previously thought to be impedimentary.

There is no mystery to transforming our schools. We already know of many successful techniques and strategies. This book has offered many others. In order for transformation to occur we need to do just three things more:

- Find the courage to begin.
- Maintain the will to persist.
- Give voice to our spirits calling for a brighter light.

APPENDIX

PLANNING FOR THE TRANSFORMATIONAL PROCESS

In order to begin a transformation process, a plan should be created. This plan should be flexible and broad. It should also be tailored to the current program, staff, and community. A successful transformation will ideally take place over the long term—as long as five years—and it will even then need to be nurtured and sustained.

It is not feasible to expect every school to think or perform in this manner. We do not subscribe to an all or nothing approach, however. There may be merit in any number of processes, any number of attempts. A full-blown, whole-school, five-year campaign may prove daunting to a principal, staff, or district. Perhaps simply beginning the One-Year Process may lead to a deeper, longer-term commitment to G/I. It is important to have a vision, but not necessarily *the* final vision in mind when the journey commences.

In the ASCD manual, *Assisting Change in Education (ACE)*, the author Ellen Saxl (with Matthew Miles and Ann Lieberman) identifies six training "modules" that encompass a range of skills considered to be essential to the G/I process. These are Trust/Rapport Building, Organizational Diagnosis, Dealing with the Process, Resource Utilization, Managing the Work, and Building the Capacity to Continue. We would suggest that all of these are key factors, and they have all been dealt with to a greater or lesser degree in this text. The skills encompassed are also evident throughout the three scenarios for tranformation outlined below. These three scenarios are all designed to begin the process, but obviously they will achieve different results in the near term.

A *One-Year Plan* might be expected simply to "plant seeds" with a traditional staff, or to break entirely new ground with an especially innovative staff. A *Three-Year Plan* might accomplish a great deal with any staff and community, so long as the G/I process still had firm commitment afterwards. With a strong and ready staff it can be thoroughly transformational. A *Five-Year Plan*, strictly adhered to, would transform virtually any school. It would all but guarantee long-term continuing transformation behavior in a strong staff within a supportive community.

Without a solid, supportive principal to coordinate the intricate process, embarking on any of these attempts will most likely prove fruitless. With a capable and committed principal, however, any of these scenarios will prove rewarding. A strong leader is essential in the transitional stages to fuller staff assumption of leadership roles.

A ONE-YEAR GROWTH/IMPROVEMENT PROCESS

Begin to Create a Climate for G/I

A. Enlist aid and support of Central Office. Share all plans and processes with appropriate people throughout the experience.

- Disseminate appropriate literature on change, middle school philosophy, and current thinking on teaching/learning.
- Be certain that staff members' annual goals are professional and focused and that their accomplishment is easily and objectively verifiable in terms of times, numbers, and dates.
- Meet in small groups or pairs to discuss the need for G/I.
- Collate data on grades, discipline referrals, dropouts, retentions, suspensions.
- Introduce a purposeful, positive tone to full staff meetings—invite all staff.
- Take exquisite care of the building and grounds.

B. Survey staff, students, and parents on aspects of the program, including academic quality, curricular clarity, goals and objectives, student/staff relations, teacher/administrator relations, climate, cleanliness, organization, etc.

- Invite outside observers to spend time in the school and share views. This could include district administrators or teachers, local college professors, someone's trusted colleague from another school system, or a consultant. If a visiting evaluation team happens to be slated for the school, take their suggestions to heart.

C. Share in a general, objective way the data and feedback that has been obtained through processes in A and B above. Look for patterns and areas of concern in the data.

- Identify regional programs worth visiting, conferences worth attending.

Go through a Process to Set Broad School Goals

A. Meet as a full staff to confirm the need for a goal-setting process. Look at current goals in light of the recently obtained data. Note incongruities of expectations and outcomes. Share modern approaches of business to the G/I process through the writings and videos of people like Covey, Peters, and Mary Beth Kantor. Include parents if that feels appropriate.

- Continue meetings of the most excited staff members. Also enable those people to meet with the dominant resisters in a non-threatening, sharing mode.

B. Begin the goal-setting process as outlined in Chapter 9.

C. Establish mutually agreed-upon, mutually developed goals for the school. Ask every staff member to sign off on those goals, if that appears beneficial.

D. Share goals with all students and parents.

Go through a Process to Set a Few Annual Goals

A. Convene committees of four to six people (in a staff of forty to sixty, six to eight in a larger staff) to discuss the need for annual goals to complement the school goals. Have those committees undertake a goal-setting process simpler than, but not unlike, the one above.

B. Establish a Teaching/Learning Committee with one representative from each of the small committees. This group with the principal as a member (initially serving as the chair unless there is some reason not to) then establish the annual goals for the remainder of the school year, as well as those goals more than likely continuing into the next year.

Improve School Climate, Student Morale, Teacher Professionalism

A. Establish a CARE Committee with another representative from the small committees, along with the administrator most responsible for student morale (who would probably serve as chair). Charge that committee with addressing concerns of student morale, beginning a CARE List, monitoring individual progress of CARE students, etc.

- Send staff to visit successful programs and to atttend regional and even national conferences, such as NMSA and ASCD. Have them share their experiences and perceptions in a full staff meeting.

B. Share pertinent information on grading, grouping, retention, etc.

- Establish a professional library of catalogued articles.
- Share current efforts with the Parent Organization, School Board, Administrative Council, etc.

C. Hold a full staff discussion on what is desirable in a new staff member. Involve many staff in any hiring decisions. Engage in a thorough, lengthy process. *Hire only superb people.*

D. Go on an end of the year retreat with as many staff as possible. Learn even more and have a darn good time!

A THREE-YEAR G/I PROCESS

Begin with the one-year process above.

Build on the First Year During the Second Year

A. Enlist continuing aid and support of Central Office. Update all plans and processes with appropriate people.

- Disseminate new literature on change, middle school philosophy, and current thinking on teaching/learning.
- Continue to ensure that staff member's annual goals are professional, focused, and easily verified.
- Meet in small groups or pairs to discuss ongoing G/I.
- Collate fresh data on grades, discipline referrals, dropouts, retentions, suspensions, etc.
- Maintain purposeful, positive tone in full staff meetings.
- Continue exquisite care of the building and grounds.

B. Re-survey staff, students, parents on aspects of program, including academic quality, curricular clarity, goals and objectives, student/staff relations, teacher/administration relations, climate, cleanliness, organization, etc.

C. Share in a general, objective way the data and feedback that has been obtained. Look for patterns, areas of concern, and areas of improvement in the data.

- Continue to identify regional programs worth visiting and conferences worth attending. Send as many staff as possible. Hold debriefing sessions afterward.

D. Improve the effectiveness of the TLC and CARE Committees.

E. Establish a schedule for bi-monthly grade level and departmental curriculum articulation meetings.

F. Adopt the Two School Rules for all members of the school community: Respect People, Respect Property.

- Dispense with cumbersome student rules and regulations.

G. Form a Citizens Advisory Committee of ten to fifteen community members, PTO officers, parents, teachers, and school administrators.

Begin Formation of Teacher Teams

A. Establish focus on importance and dynamics of teaming in in-service, annual goals, literature review, etc.

- Continue visitations to see effective teaming in action.
- Discuss teaming in full staff meetings regularly.

B. Obtain consensus for full faculty teaming, or begin teaming *Pilot(s)* through discussion and/or survey.

- Announce schedule for moving to teams—either Pilot or all.
- Survey staff on teaching subject interests, desired grade and teammates, interest in being a team leader, and suggestions of peers who would make good TLs.
- Analyze data of survey, certifications, sociograms, etc.

C. Form projected teams. Meet as teams. Begin discussion of curriculum, team process, student matters, grouping, etc.

- Continue meeting and planning as teams for purpose of functioning as teams in the third year. (Note: in our school we accomplished the planning during the first year and moved to teams in the second, rather than the third.)
- Include heavy emphasis on interdisciplinary curriculum and team dynamics.

Continue Learning, Sharing, and Publicizing

A. Continue to share pertinent information on grading, grouping, retention, etc.

- Maintain the professional library of catalogued articles.
- Share current efforts with the Parent Organization, School Board, Administrative Council, etc.

- Publicize G/I efforts through newsletter at school and district levels.
- Develop *Checklist* (Figure 12) to ensure continuity and progress on as many fronts as possible, without good things being abandoned unnecessarily.

Continue to Build Professional Staff

A. Involve many staff in any hiring decisions. Engage in a thorough, lengthy process. *Hire only superb people.*

B. Go on an *end of the year* retreat (or hold week-long workshop at least) with all projected team staff members. Develop curriculum plans for the first several months.

THE THIRD YEAR: GREAT STRIDES ARE MADE

Kaizen—Constant Improvement

A. Revisit all of the above from the previous *two* years and maintain/improve what is applicable. Examine and update *Checklist*.

B. "Feed" the Teaming process, ensure its success.

- Be certain teams have adequate, regular team planning time, daily being most appropriate.
- Develop a Team Observation Process for administrators to use in working with the teams.
- Have the Team Leader from each team be the representative on the Teaching Learning Committee.

C. Maintain and develop further consensus. Enable staff to become increasingly synergistic. Develop a lean, simple teacher handbook—or better still, no handbook.

D. Celebrate success at all levels.

- Adopt as many student recognition programs as possible.
- Adopt as many staff recognition programs as possible.
- Affirm and support all staff regularly. Most will be well on board by this time. A few may still be anxious.

E. Focus on identifying and researching *one* innovative teaching/learning strategy schoolwide. Possibilities include Cooperative Learning, Mastery Learning, Higher Order Thinking, Learning Styles, etc. Plan on beginning implementation in upcoming school year.

Begin an Advisory Program

A. Study several programs from other schools, write and visit. Share and discuss with full staff.

B. Form a committee or charge TLC with developing a format and a curriculum that will fit your program needs.

C. Share and discuss with Parent Organization and hold one or more parent forums to extoll the virtues of the plan.

(Note: Consider allowing parents to opt students out, if they cannot support the rationale. Provide homeroom/study hall experience instead for that group until whole program takes hold.)

D. Divide staff and students appropriately and make the transition to program at some logical point in the calendar—marking period, semester, or beginning of next year.

E. Monitor progress of program through committee charged with its development. Make adjustments as necessary. In time, publicize results to school and community.

Continue to Build Professional Staff

A. Involve many staff in any hiring decisions. Engage in a thorough, lengthy process. *Hire only superb people.*

B. Go on an end of the year retreat (or hold week-long workshop at least) with as many staff members as possible—everyone is ideal. Celebrate the hard work and successes of the *three-year* process. Develop consensus on the direction for the future.

A FIVE-YEAR G/I PROCESS

Begin with the one-year process above.
Build on the first year during the second year as above.
Make great strides in the third year as above.

The Fourth Year: Transformational Systems in Place

A. Revisit all of the above from the previous *three* years and maintain/improve what is applicable. Examine and update *Checklist*.

B. Continue to support the *Teaming* process, ensure its continued success.

C. Continue to support the *Advisory* program, ensure its continued success.

Building Innovation and Integrated Systems

A. Begin implementing the *one* innovative teaching/learning strategy schoolwide. Possibilities include Cooperative Learning, Mastery Learning, Higher Order Thinking, Learning Styles, etc. Develop a format similar to that used for goals, teaming, and advisory implementation.

B. Begin development of Interdisciplinary Curricular Webs in the teams. Proceed along the same transformational lines as with above G/I processes: Read, Research, Review, Do, Renew.

- Have same grade level teams compare and develop whole grade webs. Share across grades, whole school. Build possibilities, experiment, revise.

Modelling the Process for Others

A. Have staff present at workshops and conferences.

- Have staff write articles to share your G/I strategies.

B. Host district and state conferences at your site.

C. Develop attractive brochure and hand-outs on all relevant aspects of program.

D. Open your building to any and all visitors.

- Encourage visits and develop a professional format for visits.
- Provide a scenario for visitors, such as: meet with principal, tour building, spend substantial time with teams in classes and team meeting, share lunch with students and staff, conduct final debriefing with staff. Let people roam and make observations, then discuss how, why, when, etc. with them.

Continue to Build Professional Staff

A. Have teachers serve as chairpersons of TLC and CARE Committees. All members are now capable of leadership.

B. Involve all affected staff in any hiring decisions. Engage in a thorough, lengthy process. *Hire only superb people.*

C. Go on an end of the year retreat (or hold week-long workshop at least) with as many staff members as possible—everyone is ideal. Celebrate the hard work and successes of the *four-year* process. Develop consensus on the direction for the future.

THE FIFTH YEAR: WE ARE A GREAT SCHOOL

Fine Things Are Now Habitual

A. Revisit all of the above from the previous *four* years and maintain/improve what is applicable. Examine and update *Checklist.*

B. Continue to support the *Teaming* process, ensure its continued success.

C. Continue to support the *Advisory* program, ensure its continued success.

D. Continue development of the *one* innovative teaching/learning strategy schoolwide.

E. Begin identifying and researching a second teaching/learning strategy of power and purpose.

F. Continue to model the process for others, host visitors' conferences, have staff present, etc.

Create a Thoughtful, Effective Interdisciplinary Web

A. Continue development and improvement of Interdisciplinary Curricular Webs in the teams.

B. Have same grade level teams *formalize* whole-grade webs. Share across grades, whole-school.

C. Build whole-school interdisciplinary curriculum by the end of the year.

Continue to Build Professional Staff

A. Have teachers rotate as Team Leaders. All are now capable of leadership.

B. Continue to involve all affected staff in any hiring decisions. Engage in a thorough, lengthy process. *Hire only superb people.*

C. Go on an end of the year retreat (or hold week-long workshop at least) with as many staff members as possible — everyone is ideal. Celebrate the hard work and successes of the *five*-year process. Develop consensus on the direction for the future.

These are suggested formats. As with the others in this book, they are meant to serve as maps or webs, not blueprints. Look at them and use what will help you. Discard what will not. There is quite a lot here. The G/I process is not simple, especially at the beginning. The noted general manager of the great Brooklyn Dodgers teams, Branch Rickey, once said, "Luck is the residue of design." A writer on spiritual matters, H. L. Bosch, said, "Many people fail to recognize opportunity because it comes disguised as work." Jesus Christ said, "Where your treasure is, there will your heart be also."

Our children are our treasure. Our schools are the sanctuaries of our heritage and our inheritance. If we want to transform them in the most necessary sense, in the finest sense, we will need to do some serious and thoughtful planning. We will also need to do some heavy work. But above all we will need to find and fill our hearts again.

WHOLE-SCHOOL GROWTH/IMPROVEMENT CHECKLIST

Person monitoring_____   Date_____

	Begun	Ongoing	Complete
PLANTING SEEDS:			
Readings			
Discussions			
Staff meetings			
Visits			
COLLATING DATA:			
Grades			
Retentions			
Discipline referrals			
Detentions			
Suspensions			
Fights			
Attendance			
Drop-outs			
Other			
SURVEYING:			
Students			
Staff			
Parents			
GOAL-SETTING/			
CONSENSUS DEVELOPMENT:			
District			
School -- Broad			
School -- Annual			
Individual Staff -- Annual			
PLANNING:			
District			
School			
Committees			
COMMUNICATION:			
Community/Parents			
District			
School			
PROFESSIONALIZATION:			
Staff meetings			
Organization of spaces			
Appearances			
Equipment/Access			
Telephones			
Public Relations			
Emphasis on quality			
Minimal rules and regulations			
Other			
STUDENT MORALE:			
Broader grouping			
Eliminate failure			
Abolish leper colonies			
Celebrate success for all			
Alternative Learning Ctr			
Emphasis on quality			
Minimal rules and regulations			
Other			

162

	Begun	Ongoing	Complete
TEAMING:			
Survey literature			
Build consensus			
Survey staff interest			
Pilot teams			
Evaluate pilot			
Move to full teaming			
Evaluate teaming			
Modify and improve process			
Survey staff			
Continue teaming model			
Other			
SCHEDULE:			
Flexible block schedule			
Teacher control in Core blocks			
Daily team planning time			
Staggered release at each grade			
No bells			
Establish Learning Lab			
Other			
ADVISORY:			
Survey literature			
Build consensus			
Engage counseling staff			
Involve parents			
Develop curriculum			
Implement program			
Evaluate after semester/year			
Modify and improve			
Other			
INTERDISCIPLINARY CURRICULUM			
Less is more attitude			
Quality over quantity			
Study literature			
Examine desired learning outcomes			
Develop team unit building format			
Begin building webs in teams			
Evaluate			
Modify and improve			
Build units cross teams and grades			
Develop whole-school scope/sequence			
Modify and improve			
Other			
MAINTAINING THE G/I PROCESS:			
Involve staff in hiring			
Hire only superb people			
Keep goals in forefront			
Celebrate staff success			
Challenge weak staff to grow/improve			
Focused, relevant in-service			
Continually monitor all aspects			
Other			

UNIT EVALUATION

Team _____ Grade Level _____ Date _____

Title or Theme of Team Unit _____

_____

_____

Length _____ Rating _____

Subject Areas	Language Arts	Social Studies	Science	Math
Major unit objectives				
Major concepts				

Subject Areas	Language Arts	Social Studies	Science	Math
Skills developed or (*) introduced				
Behaviors or attitudes encouraged				
Principal resources				

Major interdisciplinary (team) project:_____

Minor interdisciplinary projects:_____

Rating scale: 1–5: 1 = unit not worth retaining in curriculum; 5 = all objectives achievable, fits SOL's, essential to keep, congruent with school goals.

CARE COMMITTEE STUDENT ALERT FORM

NATIONAL SCHOOL FORMS

2 Reynolds Lane, Buchanan, NY 10511

STUDENT'S NAME	**DISCIPLINARY REFERRAL**	DATE OF INCIDENT
CLASS/LOCATION	MIDDLE SCHOOL	ADVISOR/TEAM
TEACHER		PERIOD - TIME OF DAY

REASON(S) FOR THIS NOTICE:

☐ CUTTING CLASS ☐ DESTRUCTIVE TO SCHOOL PROPERTY ☐ UNACCEPTABLE LANGUAGE
☐ EXCESSIVE TARDINESS ☐ LITTERING ☐ FIGHTING
☐ LEFT GROUNDS WITHOUT PERMISSION ☐ RUDE/DISCOURTEOUS ☐ DISRUPTIVE/UNCOOPERATIVE
☐ ANNOYING TO CLASSMATES ☐ EXCESSIVE TALKING ☐ _____

ACTION TAKEN PRIOR TO THIS NOTICE:

☐ HAD CONFERENCE WITH STUDENT ☐ TEAM CONFERENCE HELD WITH STUDENT ☐ TELEPHONED PARENT
☐ CONTACTED CONFLICT MANAGER ☐ TEAM CONFERENCE HELD WITH PARENT ☐ PREVIOUS STAY IN ALC
☐ CONTACTED TEACHER ADVISOR ☐ CONTACTED GUIDANCE
☐ OTHER _____

PRESENT ACTION AND RECOMMENDATION(S):

☐ REFERRED TO CONFLICT MANAGER ☐ PARENT TELEPHONE CALL RECOMMENDED ☐ STUDENT SENT TO ALC
☐ CONFERENCE WITH STUDENT ☐ TEAM CONFERENCE RECOMMENDED ___ DAY(S) ___ PERIOD(S)
☐ STUDENT/ADVISOR CONFERENCE STUDENT/PARENT ☐ STUDENT SUSPENDED
   RECOMMENDED ☐ STUDENT PLACED ON PROBATION ☐ MATTER REFERRED TO:
☐ _____

_____ _____
(Action Taken By) *(Date)*

PINK - TEACHER'S COPY   GREEN - OFFICE COPY   GOLD - ADVISOR'S COPY

STUDENT ALERT

Date_____ Time_____

Please be advised that _____ may be in need of extra care, patience, understanding and/or supervision at this time. He/she is faced with difficulty in the following area(s):

_____ personal/family crisis

_____ possible suicidal behavior

_____ possible drug/alcohol abuse

_____ threats from other(s)

_____ illness/injury

_____ other (please specify):

_____ Contact guidance personnel as soon as possible.

_____ Additional information available in guidance office.

_____ Urgent administrative action needed.

Thank you

166

AT-RISK STUDENT LIST

School _____   Date: _____

Name	Date of Birth	G.P.A.	Grade(s) Retained	# Office Referrals	# Times I.S.S.	# Times O.S.S.	On Court Probation?	# Days Tardy	# Days Missed	Major Trauma?	Alcohol/ Drug Abuse?	Sp. Ed. Label?	Improved? + – o

LETTER OF COMMENDATION

Student Name (print) _____ Date _____

Teacher/Administrator (print) _____

The items checked below indicate *exceptional behavior* in that area.
Your child may also be performing quite well in most or all other areas
listed without that being *officially* noted in this way.

ATTITUDE
____ friendliness
____ courtesy/respect
____ cooperation
____ appearance
____ open-mindedness
____ persistence
____ citizenship
____ honesty/trustworthiness
____ manners/consideration of
    others
____ willingness to try new things
____ humor/enjoyment of the
    learning process
____ significant improvement in
    attitude/behavior
____ other _____
    _____
____ other _____
    _____

ATTENDANCE
____ regular attendance
____ attentiveness
____ concentration
____ getting to class on time
____ other _____
    _____

PRODUCTIVITY
____ effort
____ preparation for class
____ classroom participation
____ neat, attractive work
____ following through on
    assignments
____ doing more than required
____ significant academic
    progress
____ other _____
    _____

COMMENTS: _____

_____

_____

Signature _____

168

MIDDLE SCHOOL SCHEDULE: Block, Period, Rotational

Grades 5 and 6

8:15				11:10	11:55	12:55	1:50
Period	1	2	3	4	5	6*	7**
XX ADV	C	O R	E	Lunch/Recess	CORE	EX/Band	PE
YY ADV	C	O R	E	Recess/Lunch	CORE	PE	EX/Orch

(Release to buses 2:35)

Grade 7

8:15			10:25	11:20	12:15	1:00		1:50
Period	1	2	3	4*	5	6		7**
X ADV	C	O R E	PE	EL/Band	Lun/Social	C	O R	E
Y ADV	C	O R E	EL/Orch	PE	Lun/Social	C	O R	E

(Release to buses 2:38)

Grade 8

8:15	8:20	9:10	10:00	10:50	11:50	12:15	1:05	1:55
Period	1	2*	3	4	5	6	7	8**
X ADV	EL/Orch	PE	C O R E		Lunch	C O R E		EL
Y ADV	PE	EL/Band	C O R E		Lunch	C O R E		EL

(Release to buses 2:40)

Notes: X & Y = Teams of Students (75-100)
CORE = language arts, mathematics, science and social studies
ADV = Advisory, meets every day in homeroom 10 minutes 5-7, 5 minutes 8
** also meets last period once per week
PE = Physical Education/Health, meets every day (except 6th grade ADV time)
EX = Exploratory Arts--Art, Music, Technology, Home Ec., etc.quarter/semester, different courses for 5th and 6th graders
EL = Electives-- Art, Tech, HEC, Comput, For. Lang., etc., semester/full year
*also provides for Chorus/Activity/SSR period every third day, switch at semester to opposite period
All teachers have four classes, team and individual planning, duty/ fifth class daily

169

Possible Schedule Times

CORE Times

Grade	Approximate minutes per week
5th	1100
6th	1115
7th	1150
8th	1000

Lunch/Flex Times

Grade	Lunch	Flex
5th	11:55-12:16	12:16-12:35
6th	12:18-12:38	11:58-12:18
7th	10:53-11:08	10:35-10:53
8th	11:15-11:45	Fewer auxiliary spaces available

Activity Periods

Grade	Day	Time
5th	Tuesday	1:40-2:32
6th	Wednesday	12:40-1:35
7th	Wednesday	9:45-10:30
8th	Wednesday	9:45-10:30

Block Schedule Area Code

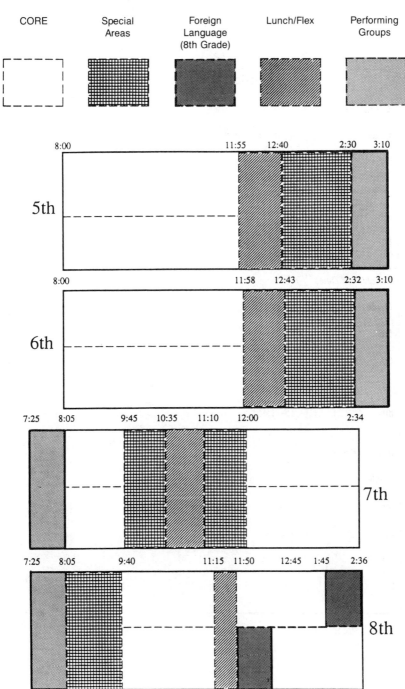

CORE | Special Areas | Foreign Language (8th Grade) | Lunch/Flex | Performing Groups

171

GLOSSARY

Acceleration The practice of skipping previously retained students up a grade level in order to catch them up to their social peers.

Additional Experience Option An opportunity to provide optional enrichment for students with specific interests, such as labelled Gifted and Talented students (though not restricted to that group), either during the school day at special times and/or as an after-school program.

Advisory A schoolwide program in which each teacher establishes a mentoring relationship with a group of ten to fifteen students and monitors their progress for a year or more. The group meets every day in a homeroom setting and also frequently as a group devoted to special activities drawn from an advisory curriculum as well as from unique staff and student interests.

Alternative Learning Center A program to replace traditional in-school suspension tanks with a teaching/learning environment designed to enable the student to successfully return to the regular school setting. For optimal impact, ALC is coordinated and staffed by a certified professional.

Balance An attitude or perspective that emphasizes wholeness, congruence, and complementarity, rather than dichotomy and either/or thinking.

Block Schedule A scheduling pattern in which one or more blocks of time substantially larger than the typical period are provided for a team of teachers and students to use each day as the teachers determine.

CARE Committee A representative group of staff charged with identifying, monitoring, and assisting Children At Risk Educationally.

Conditional Pass A means of enabling a struggling student under extreme circumstances of duress, who is clearly able to accomplish acceptable work, to complete a course that normally he/she would have to repeat.

Consensus The process by which everyone in the group is finally able to support the decision and the direction of the group.

Constrained Worldview   A belief that there really is not enough of the essentials of life (material goods, physical space, intelligence, success, love, etc.) to go around.

CORE Curriculum   The combining of the traditionally essential subjects of language arts, social studies, mathematics, and science into a common Core experience for a team of teachers and students. Such an approach is more or less effective to the degree of curricular integration or interdisciplinarity.

Dichotomy   A position of unavoidable, irreversible difference.

Engagement   Involvement in something to the degree that one is still talking about it at dinner time.

Exploratories   Mini-courses primarily in the arts and technology areas designed to provide younger students with a sampling of a subject prior to their choosing longer elective courses later in their middle school years.

Grouping   The placing of students together based on comparable ability, performance, and other factors, but only for a particular class or two each day—generally language arts/reading, and/or math.

Growth/Improvement   A synonym for positive, substantive, lasting change.

Interdisciplinary Curriculum   Developing curriculum so that it is integrated among several disciplines or more through common themes or topics. There are many varieties of interdisciplinary curricula—from a two- or three-discipline combination such as the language arts/social studies/fine arts humanities-type unit or approach, to a whole-school integrated day in which interdisciplinary student project work over long and flexible blocks of time is a predominant activity.

Kaizen   A notion taken from the Japanese of "constant improvement" as a personal and organizational goal.

Learning Lab   A remedial program designed to replace traditional remedial classrooms of ten to twenty underachieving students and one teacher in a drill and practice mode, with a holistic, supportive, user-friendly teaching/learning environment of three to five students with one teacher, or six to ten students with one teacher and an assistant, in an individualized or small group tutorial mode related directly to CORE classroom experiences.

Leper Colonies   Organized groupings of student misfits, outcasts, or under-achievers in the school. Examples are large remedial classes of the type replaced by the Learning Lab, detention halls, vocational education classes, low-level tracked classes, in-school suspension pits, etc.

Less Presently-Capable Student   A more positive, optimistic way of categorizing underachieving students, with the assumption that "intelligence" is not finite, stagnant, or quantifiable. (Those few students with severe intellectual or emotional dysfunctions are a different matter, although even these may show dramatic improvement in transformational school settings.)

Metasubject The traditional academic disciplines of English, mathematics, social studies, science, and foreign language when they are taught in a square body/fat head, terminal teaching mode that makes the experience in all the classes essentially the same for students.

More Presently-Capable Student A broader, more equitable way of categorizing students we typically label bright or gifted, with the assumption that "intelligence" is not finite, stagnant, or quantifiable.

Person-Centered Approach A humane and functional way of dealing with all people in the school, demonstrating that staff and students have an equal stake in the quality of the day-to-day experience. This is superior to the "staff-centered" approach dominant in many schools and also to the "child-centered" approach devised to counteract it.

Process/Product The notion that process and product are so interrelated as to be inseparable. There will be no quality product without quality process, and vice versa.

Role-Freeze A way of seeing school people as specialists only responsible for specific areas of school operation and success, rather than seeing everyone as key players ultimately responsible for team success.

Student Morale Considering student discipline issues and statistics holistically, as reflective of the general quality of student life in the school. If student morale is poor, student discipline will be troublesome. If student morale is high, discipline will not be problematic. Therefore, look at ways to improve morale, rather than enforce discipline.

Square Body/Fat Head A traditional spatial and intellectual classroom arrangement in which the teacher is predominant physically and mentally, and the students are expected to function as obedient little boxes in a larger box.

Teaching/Learning The notion that teaching and learning are so interrelated as to be inseparable. This is in contrast to the currently popular terminology of "delivery of instruction," for teaching, and "coverage of content" for learning.

Team Observation Process A systematic, whole team, observation and consultation experience in which an administrator spends a week or more with a team of teachers. The focus is on mutually determined areas of interest in classrooms, team meetings, and in individual teacher-administrator conferences.

Teaming Placing two or more teachers together with a set group of students for an entire year. Often teaming involves the CORE curriculum teachers, with special area teachers in a support role, although many variations are possible. Teaming requires regular team planning and may also involve team teaching, although not necessarily.

Terminal Teaching   The standard procedure in which all thinking in a classroom basically begins and ends with the teacher. The teacher and the teacher's viewpoint and style are domineering. The teacher is responsible for "motivating" the students. When viewed in terms of total mental efficiency, this procedure is seen as woefully lacking.

Terminus Teaching   A synergistic process/product by which all people in the class are fully involved. Although the teacher is the recognized authority in many areas and the most mature person in the room, all are encouraged to take responsibility for their own motivation in the teaching/learning setting. Therefore thoughts begin and end in a variety of places and brains, with both predictable and unpredictable outcomes.

Tracking   Grouping all students based on comparable ability, performance, or related measures and keeping them together in virtually all classes all day long.

Transescence   The developmental period when the young person moves from childhood to early adolescence. This occurs approximately between the ages of ten and fourteen for girls, and eleven and fifteen for boys.

Transescents   People in transescence.

Transformation   An ongoing process/product by which a school community becomes far more humane, productive, thoughtful, and engaging for all people involved.

Unconstrained Worldview   A belief that there really is enough of the essentials of life (material goods, physical space, intelligence, success, love, etc.) to go around.

Whole-School   The perspective that views everything happening in the school in totality, as part of a larger whole, and therefore both related to, and responsive to, that greater whole. With this perspective, all attempts at growth/improvement are seen in the larger context, with many attempts proceeding simultaneously, and all people part of the G/I process/product.

BIBLIOGRAPHY

Adler, M. 1984. *The Paidea Program: An Educational Syllabus*. New York: Macmillan.

Ball, K. 1991. "Fifty Per Cent of Teens Not Ready for Work, U.S. Panel Says," Survey of Study by Labor Secretary's Commission on Achieving Necessary Skills, *Philadelphia Inquirer*, June 28, 1991.

Bennis, W. and B. Nanus. 1985. *Leaders: The Strategies for Taking Charge*. New York: Harper and Row.

Berliner, D. 1985. "Does Ability Grouping Cause More Problems Than It Solves?" *Instructor and Teacher*, 94(8):14–15.

Boyer, E. 1983. *High School: A Report on Secondary Education in America*. New York: Harper and Row.

Brandt, R. 1987. "On Cooperation in Schools: A Conversation with David and Roger Johnson," *Educational Leadership*, 45(3):14–19.

Brandt, R. 1988. "What Should Schools Teach," in *Content of the Curriculum*, R. Brandt, ed., Alexandria, VA: Association for Supervision and Curriculum Development, pp. 1–8.

Brandt, R., ed. 1989. *Conversations with Leading Educators*. Alexandria, VA: Association for Supervision and Curriculum Development.

Bray, A. 1979. "Evaluating and Selecting Programs for Gifted, Talented Students," *NASSP Bulletin*, 63(438).

Canady, R. L. and Phyliss A. Hotchkiss. 1990. "It's a Good Score, Just a Bad Grade," *Phi Delta Kappan*. 71(7):662–665.

Caine, R. N. and Geoffrey Caine. 1991. *Making Connections: Teaching and the Human Brain*. Alexandria, VA: ASCD.

Carrol, J. 1990. "The Copernican Plan: Restructing the American High School," *Phi Delta Kappan*, 71(5):358–365.

Center for Policy Research in Education. 1989. "Repeating Grades in School: Current Practice and Research Evidence," CPRE, Rutgers University, New Brunswick, NJ.

Champlin, J. 1987. "Leadership: A Change Agent's View," in *Leadership: Examining the Elusive*, Alexandria, VA: Association for Supervision and Curriculum Development, pp. 49–63.

Covey, S. 1989. *The 7 Habits of Highly Effective People: Powerful Lessons in Personal Change*. New York; Simon and Schuster.

Dyer, W. 1989. *You'll See It When You Believe It: The Way to Your Personal Transformation*. New York: Avon Books.

Eisner, E. 1985. *The Educational Imagination*. 2nd Edition. New York: Macmillan.

Elkind, D. 1980. "Investigating Intelligence in Early Adolescence," in *Toward Adolescence: The Middle School Years*. M. Johnson, ed., Chicago: University of Chicago Press.

Emerson, R. W. 1965. *Essays, First Series*. Vol. 2 of *The Complete Works of Ralph Waldo Emerson*. Horace E. Concord, ed., Boston: Houghton Mifflin, pp. 1903–1904.

Freire, P. 1957. *The Pedagogy of the Oppressed*. New York: Continuum.

Gardner, H. 1985. *Frames of Mind: The Theory of Multiple Intelligences*. New York: Basic Books.

George, P. 1983. *The Theory Z School: Beyond Effectiveness*. Columbus, OH: National Middle School Association.

George, P. 1988. "What's the Truth about Tracking and Ability Grouping Really???" Gainesville, FL: Teacher Education Resources.

George, P. and W. Anderson. 1989. "Maintaining the Middle School: A National Survey," *NASSP BULLETIN*. December, Reston, VA: NASSP.

Glasser, W. 1990. *The Quality School*. New York: Harper and Row.

Glatthorn, A. and N. Spencer. 1986. *Middle School/Junior High Principal's Handbook*. Englewood Cliffs, NJ: Prentice Hall.

Goodlad, J. 1983. *A Place Called School: Prospects for the Future*. New York: McGraw Hill.

Gould, S. J. 1985. *The Mismeasure of Man*. New York: Alfred Knopf.

Hammer, R. 1983. "The Immorality of Ability Level Tracking," *English Journal*, 92(1):40.

Hart, L. 1986. "A Response: All Thinking Paths Lead to the Brain," *Educational Leadership*, 42(8):45–48.

Hawking, S. 1988. *A Brief History of Time: From the Big Bang to Black Holes*. New York: Bantam.

Heward, W. L. and Michael D. Orlansky. 1984. *Exceptional Children*. Columbus, OH: Charles Merril.

Hilliard, A. G., III. 1991. Address to Fourth General Session, ASCD Annual Conference, San Francisco, CA, March 17, 1991.

Iacocca, L. 1991. Address to the Second General Session, ASCD Annual Conference, San Francisco, CA, March 15, 1991.

Jacobs, H., ed. 1989. *Interdisciplinary Curriculum: Design and Implementation*. Alexandria, VA: Association for Curriculum and Supervision Development.

Johnson, D., Edythe Holubec, and Roger Johnson. 1986. *Circles of Learning: Cooperation in the Classroom*. Edina, MN: Interaction.

Johnston, H. and G. Markle. 1982. *What Research Says to the Middle Level Practitioner*. Columbus, OH: National Middle School Association.

Kagan, S. 1989. *Cooperative Learning: Resources for Teachers*. San Juan Capistrano, CA: Resources for Teachers.

Kohn, A. 1991. "Caring Kids: The Role of the Schools," *Phi Delta Kappan*, 72(7):496–506.

Lipsitz, J. 1980. *Growing Up Forgotten: A Review of Research and Programs Concerning Early Adolescence*. New Brunswick, NJ: Transaction.

Machado, L. A. 1980. *The Right to Be Intelligent*. New York: Pergamon Press.

Martin, L. and B. Pavan. 1976. "Current Research on Open Space, Nongrading, Vertical Grouping, and Team Teaching," *Phi Delta Kappan*, 57(5):310–314.

McCluhan, M. and Quentin Fiore. 1965. *The Medium Is the Massage: An Inventory of Effects*. New York: Bañtam.

McGinitie, W. 1991. "Reading Instruction: Plus Ca Change . . .," *Educational Leadership*, 48(6):55–58.

Merton, T. 1965. *The Way of Chuang Tzu*. New York: New Directions.

Moyers, B. 1989. *A World of Ideas: Conversations with Thoughtful Men and Women about American Life Today and the Ideas Shaping Our Future*, Betty Sue Flowers, ed., New York: Doubleday.

Naisbitt, J. 1986. 6th Edition. *Megatrends: Ten New Directions Transforming Our Lives*. New York: Warner Books.

Oakes, J. 1981. "The Reproduction of Inequality: The Content of Secondary School Tracking," *The Urban Review*, 14(2):116–118.

Oakes, J. 1985. *Keeping Track: How Schools Structure Inequality*. New Haven, CT: Yale University Press.

Peck, M. S. 1987. *The Different Drum: Community Making and Peace*. New York: Simon and Schuster.

Peters, T. 1988. *Thriving on Chaos: Handbook for a Management Revolution*. New York: Harper and Row.

Phillips, D. and J. Soltis. 1985. *Perspectives on Learning*. New York: Teachers College Press.

Raebeck, B. 1987. "Secondary School Reform: Tinkering with an Obsolete Engine," *Contemporary Education*, 58(4):186–191.

Raebeck, B. 1987. *Toward a Process Model for a High School Classroom*. Ann Arbor, MI: VMI.

Raebeck, B. 1990. "Transformation of a Middle School," *Educational Leadership*, 47(7):18–21.

Raebeck, B. and C. Beegle. 1988. "Synthesystem: A New Organizational Model for Secondary School," *NASSP Bulletin*, 72(506).

Saxl, E., M. Miles, and A. Lieberman. 1989. *Assisting Change in Education*. Alexandria, VA: ASCD.

Sheive, L. and M. Schoenheit. 1987. "Vision and the Work Life of Educational Leaders," in *Leadership: Examining the Elusive*. Alexandria, VA: Association for Supervision and Curriculum Development.

Shepard, L. and M. Smith, eds. 1989. *Flunking Grades: Research and Policies on Retention*. London: Falmer Press.

Shepard, L. and M. Smith. 1990. "Synthesis of Research on Grade Retention," *Educational Leadership*, 42(8):84–88.

Silberman, C. 1970. *Crisis in the Classroom: The Remaking of American Education*. New York: Random House.

Sizer, T. 1984. *Horace's Compromise: The Dilemma of the American High School.* Boston: Houghton Mifflin.

Slavin, R. 1990. *Cooperative Learning: Theory, Research and Practice.* Englewood Cliffs, NJ: Prentice Hall.

Smith, F. 1990. *To Think.* New York: Teachers College Press.

Smith, W. and R. Andrews. 1989. *Instructional Leadership: How Principals Make a Difference.* Alexandria, VA: Association for Supervision and Curriculum Development.

Steele, Shelby. 1990. *The Content of Our Character: A New Vision of Race in America.* New York: St. Martin's Press.

Sternberg, R. 1985. *Beyond Intelligence: A Triarchic Theory of Human Intelligence.* New York: Cambridge University Press.

Sternberg, R. and T. Lubart. 1991. "Creating Creative Minds," *Phi Delta Kappan*, 72(8):608–614.

U.S. Department of Education. 1987. *What Works: Research about Teaching and Learning*, 2nd Edition. Pueblo, CO.

Whitehead, A. N. 1929. *The Aims of Education and Other Essays*. New York: Macmillan.

Wilson, B. and D. Schmits. 1978. "What's New in Ability Grouping?" *Phi Delta Kappan*, 59(8):535–536.

INDEX

ABOUT THE AUTHOR

Barry Raebeck has been actively involved in educational transformation for many years. He has been a public school teacher, principal, counselor, and central office administrator. Dr. Raebeck has consulted with school districts and universities throughout the East. He has published articles in *Educational Leadership, NASSP Bulletin, Education Digest*, and *The Clearinghouse*, among others. Dr. Raebeck is also a regular participant in national conferences and workshops. Middle-level transformation is an area of particular interest and expertise, as Dr. Raebeck has personally led such transformation at the classroom, school, and district level. He is a former member of the Virginia Middle School Task Force, and the middle school program he designed and led as principal in Harrisonburg, Virginia, was both featured on a University of Virginia regional telecast and recognized as exemplary by ASCD in 1989. Dr. Raebeck has taught for the University of Virginia, Penn State University, and Cabrini College in Radnor, Pennsylvania. He currently is Supervisor of the Arts, Social Studies, and Technology for Tredyffrin/Easttown Schools in Berwyn, PA. A major involvement of his is the district's transition to middle schools.

Dr. Raebeck believes that the central issues of transformation are joy, quality, imagination, and spirit. Without these elements, too many of our efforts will prove ineffectual, and too many of our schools will remain mediocre.